12 —

POETIC PILGRIMAGE

POETIC PILGRIMAGE

AN ESSAY IN EDUCATION

By

B. C. DILTZ, M.A.

KENNIKAT PRESS
Port Washington, N. Y./London

POETIC PILGRIMAGE

First published in 1942
Reissued in 1970 by Kennikat Press
Library of Congress Catalog Card No: 73-105780
ISBN 0-8046-0949-7

Manufactured by Taylor Publishing Company   Dallas, Texas

A DEDICATION

To all those boys and girls and men and women who, as pupils or as student-teachers, have through the years been my good companions on this pilgrimage, I dedicate this book in partial acknowledgement of their good-will.

FOREWORD

For many people aesthetic experience plays an insignificant part in the drama of human action. This book attempts to disclose some of the values that may be contributed by the art of poetry to the art of living. In a world at war it may appear irrelevant, if not impertinent, to speak of poetry, but the fact is the inception of the theme of this book goes back to the first Great War and its application may help, in a very small way, to prevent the development of another world war.

Most of the books on literary method and criticism that have appeared in the past thirty years have, in one way or another, and sometimes through over-simplification, arrived at disintegration and dissolution.

> All we have gained, then, by our unbelief
> Is a life of doubt diversified by faith
> For one of faith diversified by doubt.[1]

"Scientific" analysis, adapted to the study of literature, has been made an end in itself. The purpose has been to break down a whole into its parts; very little thought has been given to the considerable task of making a synthesis of the parts. This attitude has become a fashion characteristic of the thought of our time. Not only the historian and the literary critic, but the psychologist and the educationist as well have been studiously or inadvertently reducing life and literature to its lowest common denominator. Divide and subdivide in order the more

[1] Robert Browning, *Bishop Blougram's Apology.*

conveniently to subdue and control! This procedure
has brought about a disintegrating and dissembling
scholarship, and the consequent need for a managerial
administration and a form of regimentation that confines
rather than liberates the spirit. This process, traced to its
conclusion, ends in decadence and decay, disillusionment
and impotence, in "a freedom synonymous with
damnation". Chaos is likely to ensue when the powers
of imagination, intellect, and will are confused. The
residue of this exhaustion is the artificiality of a false
intellectualism.

The chief aim of *Poetic Pilgrimage* is to suggest one
way by which to reverse this process—to bring order out
of chaos. It aims to show by practice how the analysable
parts of poetry may be unified and co-ordinated, integrated
and synthesized, into an effective whole. It does not aim
to reduce poetry to its separate ingredients in order to
teach these parts to mystified pupils. It does not aim to
give false comfort to the perishing while others seek in
vain for security, guidance, and training. It does not aim
to offer satisfaction at the lowest levels; but it does aim to
give leadership to all the pupils in a class by leading the
more earnest of them, and by accepting the fact that
some are born to follow and can learn best and serve best
as followers. The experiencing of literature, like that of
life, may be common to all, but it should never be
commonplace. It is something unique, without price.
What must be reached for, awakens interest and quickens
effort. In the presence of an interested teacher, interest
is infectious. Even the followers, who were once proffered
literary sawdust, may now, from time to time taste of the

good fruit of literature, and perchance by tasting, quicken their sense of taste. Method is necessary. *Poetic Pilgrimage* aims to build a synthesis of life and literature, of living and reading, and to make the whole process of education in literature constructive, creative, and qualitative.

This is the main claim that this book makes to originality. Perhaps never before has the *teaching* of English, both as literary heritage and as living language, appeared so necessary and important as it does today. Should education become an instrument of political expedience and patronage, the study of literature will be no more than a title for the propaganda of the demagogue. It will, indeed, teach itself! How vain it is to lecture pupils and students on the amenities of reading when they really wish to learn how to read! How wasteful of human life to leave them to struggle helplessly in a wide morass of bluff and balderdash, for the sake of maintaining a false sense of liberty. When the smoke of gloomy ideologies has been blown out of the sky, the sunlit pastures of true freedom may be again restored to man. But if ever we are to surmount the dangers and difficulties of life's pilgrimage to this promised land, the spirit of youth must be tempered to cut through the underbrush of hypocrisy that chokes the way. Too much sympathy has been wasted on callous skeptics. Too much importance has been attached to their stubborn mental reservations. We have been too long imprudently patient with mediocrity, incompetence, and sentimentality masquerading as scholarship. Confounded by the religious arrogance of nineteenth century pietism, we have tolerated too long the shrewdness, adroitness, and duplicity that have flourished under its protection. Consequently, the will to justice has been superseded by the will to power. Deceived by twentieth-century conventionism we have closed our eyes to the corruption and wily "leadership" of unctuous self-seekers. Freedom of thought has unfortunately become identified with "free-thought". *Poetic Pilgrimage* is an attempt to open again the way to genuine liberty and truth.

At the end of this book a list of the most valuable materials consulted in the preparation of this manuscript has been appended for the guidance of the reader. Every one of these books will well repay the time and effort of any one interested in this subject. Every one of them makes its meaning clear and terse, avoiding, on the one hand, the sophistication of big words and, on the other, the affectation of little ones.

A first draft of *Poetic Pilgrimage* was submitted to Dr. J. E. Althouse, Dean of the Ontario College of Education, and to Professor H. R. MacCallum, Department of Philosophy, University College, University of Toronto. To these gentlemen, for their valuable criticism and candid advice, I am deeply grateful.

Finally, I gratefully acknowledge the kindness of authors (or their executors) and of publishers in granting me permission to include copyright passages in this book.

B. C. D.

CONTENTS

POETIC PILGRIMAGE

Chapter One

POETRY AND BELIEF

BELIEF

AT a time when the chief interest of man seems to be centred in a material world, what function, if any, has poetry in the life of a people? What contribution can literature, as one form of aesthetic experience, make to the mental life of the trained reader and through him to the formation of the beliefs by which a nation lives? Momentous changes in our attitudes have already taken place, more appear on the horizon, and a new set of presuppositions, without which we cannot very well live together as a people, is already taking shape. It may require years to reap the benefits in education, but in furthering the process by which a new philosophy of education is evolved the part that can be played by the study of literature as an art for the sake of experience is so important at the secondary school level that an understanding and appreciation of its nature is a duty incumbent on every teacher of the subject. What hope is there for the pupil, if the teacher does not know where he is going? The views set forth below are not intended to be answers to the questions asked above. They are expressed with the hope that in both substance and style they may awaken thought and provoke discussion before it is too late.

Fortunately, it is possible today to deal with the uses of poetry without appearing to plead a special case. The other arts have likewise suffered and survived. The present

3

crisis in our beliefs is already near its climax, and the course by which we are to reach our goal is already, despite the anguish of its tortuous way, resounding to the tramp of many feet. Looking ahead we cannot see very far into the mist, but looking back we can trace quite clearly the course by which we have come. "With a mirror of brass you can adjust your hat," so runs the proverb, "but with antiquity for a mirror you can predict the rise and fall of empires." But the aim of this chapter is not to gaze into some magic crystal to read the future; it is simply to find out whence we have recently come to our present impasse, in the hope, perhaps vain, that we may determine whither we are immediately going. Half way to the solution of any problem is the discovery of what caused it to be a problem.

The date 1453 is convenient. Since that time there is abundant evidence that, in spite of the widespread establishment of universities, libraries, and laboratories for the extension of learning and discovery, man has thought more and more of himself and less of God. To what end, it may be asked, does all this advancement of science and expansion of knowledge lead—to the glory of God or to the glorification of man? At the beginning of the Renaissance a conception of man as a so-called emancipated individual got itself implanted in the heads of men, and it is the cultivated fruit from the pruned growth of that distant seed that we are gathering today. The name by which the identity of this growth has been preserved is the cult of humanism. It matters not by what name it is qualified—classical, romantic, Christian, or pagan—humanism remains in its fundamental conception the same—anthropocentric. Originally it was a splendid vision intended to serve a noble purpose—a means to an end; but since the Renaissance it has deteriorated until today, its original form only faintly recognizable, it is rotten at the core. It is, indeed, an end in itself.

But it is possible to show, I think, that all thought since the Renaissance, in spite of its apparent variety, in reality forms one coherent whole. It all rests on the same presuppositions which were denied by the previous period. It all rests on the same conception of the nature of man, and all exhibits the same complete inability to realize the meaning of the dogma of Original Sin. In this period not only has its philosophy, its literature, and its ethics been based on this new conception of man as fundamentally good, as sufficient, as the measure of things, but a good case can even be made out for regarding many of its characteristic economic features as springing entirely from this central abstract conception.[1]

All that has devolved from "this central abstract conception" may be traced back to the shift of emphasis from the significance of God to the rights of man. Down the centuries this emphasis has been fitfully increased until man has become thoroughly emancipated—freed of everything but his own self-sufficiency. "Humanism is the effort of men to think, to feel, and to act for themselves, and to abide by the logic of results."[2] But, perhaps, contrast affords a clearer means of definition.

It would perhaps have been better to have avoided the word religious, as that to the 'emancipated' man at once suggests something exotic, or mystical, or some sentimental reaction. I am not, however, concerned so much with religion, as with the attitude, the 'way of thinking', the categories, from which a religion springs, and which often survive it. While this attitude tends to find expression in myth, it is independent of myth; it is, however, much

[1] T. E. Hulme, *Speculations; Essays on Humanism and the Philosophy of Art* (ed. Read). Kegan Paul, 1924.
[2] G. Scott, *The Architecture of Humanism*. Constable, 1924.

more intimately connected with dogma. For the purposes of this discussion, the bare minimum without any expression in religion is sufficient, the abstract categories alone. I want to emphasise that this attitude is a possible one for the 'emancipated' and 'reasonable' man at this moment. I use the word religious, because as in the past the attitude has been the source of most religions, the word remains convenient.

A.—The Religious attitude: (1) . . . Ethical values are *not* relative to human desires and feelings, but absolute and objective . . . Religion supplements this . . . by its conception of *Perfection*. (2) In the light of these absolute values, man himself is judged to be essentially limited and imperfect. He is endowed with Original Sin. While he can occasionally accomplish acts which partake of perfection, he can never himself *be* perfect. Certain secondary results in regard to ordinary human action in society follow from this. A man is essentially bad, he can only accomplish anything of value by discipline—ethical and political. Order is thus not merely negative, but creative and liberating. Institutions are necessary.

B.—The Humanist attitude: When a sense of the reality of these absolute values is lacking, you get a refusal to believe any longer in the radical imperfection of either Man or Nature. This develops logically into the belief that life is the source and measure of all values, and that man is fundamentally good. Instead, then, of

Man (radically imperfect) . . . apprehending . . . Perfection,— you get the second term (now entirely misunderstood) illegitimately introduced inside the first. This leads to a complete change in all values. The problem of evil disappears, the conception of sin loses all meaning. Man may be that bastard thing, 'a harmonious character.' Under ideal conditions, everything of value will spring spontaneously from free 'personalities.' If nothing good seems to appear spontaneously now, that is because of external restrictions and obstacles. Our political ideal should be the removal of everything that checks the 'spontaneous growth of personality.' Progress is thus possible, and order is a merely negative conception.

The errors which follow from this confusion of things which ought to be kept separate are of two kinds. The true nature both of the human and the Divine is falsified.

(1) The error in human things; the confusion blurs the clear outlines of human relations by introducing into them the Perfection that properly belongs to the non-human . . .

(2) The confusion created in the absolute values of religion and ethics is even greater. It distorts the real nature of ethical values by deriving them out of essentially subjective things, like desires and feelings; and all attempts to 'explain' religion, on a humanist basis, whether it be Christianity, or an alien religion like Buddhism, must always be futile. As a minor example of this, take the question of immortality. It seems paradoxical at first sight, that the Middle Ages, which lacked entirely the conception of personality, had a real belief in immortality; while thought since the Renaissance, which has been dominated by the belief in personality, has not had the same conviction. You might have expected that it would be the people who thought they really had something worth preserving who would have thought they were immortal, but the contrary is the case.[1]

Between the two extremes contrasted in this passage there lies a world of difference. They face in opposite directions, but when juxtaposed they are full of meaning. The religious man, the believer in the Everlasting God, humbly accepts the fact that he is by nature imperfect and incapable of perfection, and strains constantly to see through the mists that surround him the light that comes from above. Believing that God is the primary cause of religious faith, he acknowledges Him as the supreme and absolute authority in the world of man. To His Will all other values are relative. Believing that creation is controlled from above and not from beneath, by God and not by man, he makes distinction between things human and things divine. He tries to understand and express the meaning and implication of the command "Render unto Caesar the things that are Caesar's, and unto God the things that are God's." Believing in the atoning power of Jesus Christ, he cheerfully takes up his Cross and dedicates himself to His service. From this point of view he tries

[1] *Speculations; Essays on Humanism and the Philosophy of Art.*

to make the best of life, believing not only that faith without works is dead, but also that work without faith is lifeless. He is a man and not a god; but he also knows that man is essentially a spiritual creature and may, by the grace of God, become a St. Paul, a St. Francis, a Shakespeare, or a Lincoln.

> For thence,—a paradox
> Which comforts while it mocks,—
> Shall life succeed in that it seems to fail:
> What I aspired to be,
> And was not, comforts me:
> A brute I might have been, but would not sink i' the scale.[1]

For the completion of himself, it seems inevitable that man should reach for something beyond himself. The religious man knows that mere human intelligence alone is insufficient for his needs. So many different forms of religion have served the groping hand of man that no further proof is necessary of his unhappy feeling of incompleteness, or imperfection, and, at the same time, of the restless urge within him to achieve a destiny forever veiled from view. To this urge the saint, the warrior, and the poet all bear witness. It is intuitive to aspire, and the scope of the religious man's aspirations is infinite. This is the true freedom on which all other genuine freedoms depend. The religious man keeps first things first. He believes that Christianity is still the greatest challenge to the spirit of man. The humanist, on the other hand, has all his needs within his grasp or at least within his power of calculation and manipulation. He believes that man is sufficient unto himself and is responsible primarily to his own will. Paradoxically this leads to the law of the

---

[1] Robert Browning, *Rabbi Ben Ezra.*

jungle—to the selfishness, jealousy, prejudice, and inhumanity that breed war, famine, and disease.

The Ideal Man of the eighteenth century was the Rationalist; of the seventeenth, the Christian Stoic; of the Renaissance, the Free Individual; of the Middle Ages, the Contemplative Saint. And what is our Ideal Man? On what grand and luminous mythological figure does contemporary humanity attempt to model itself? The question is embarrassing. Nobody knows. And, in spite of all the laudable efforts of the Institute for Intellectual Co-operation to fabricate an acceptable Ideal Man for the use of Ministers of Education, nobody, I suspect, will know until such time as a major poet appears upon the scene with the unmistakable revelation. Meanwhile, one must be content to go on piping up for reason and realism and a certain decency.[1]

From Contemplative Saint to Free Individual, to Christian Stoic, and thence to Rationalist—thus runs the course by which we have come. In the piping note with which this passage ends there is a pathetic tone of impending defeat, if not despair. When a man shifts the focus of his trust from God to his own self-sufficient intellect, he becomes what may be called, for want of a better word, an intellectual—a person who puts his confidence in his own proud and infallible reason alone, as he gropes his way through the wilderness of his senses.

From rationalism to intellectualism is a perfectly natural descent. Again and again down the years weary voices had proclaimed that something had gone wrong with man's thinking—that some of the philosophers had lost their heads. But there was no turning back. The forward rush was reckless, without insight—a surge of Utopian dreaming without solid vision. Rousseau, with his audacious schemes, was a pioneer in self-centred

[1] Aldous Huxley, *Texts and Pretexts*. Chatto and Windus, 1932.

humanism. So was Marx in his time with his materialistic
theories of the rights of man. But what early humanist
could have dreamed that his cult would one day liberate
the intellectual who has in recent years sought to reduce
man's potentialities to the narrow confines of the human
intellect, or the emotionalist whose unintelligent optimism
and ineffectual love of this spacious world find expression
in a toleration of everything? Some evidence of the
narrowness of the intellectuals' point of view may be
found in the recent furious development of the study of
psychology. This pseudo-science attempts to apply to man
the scientific methods applicable to the study of matter—
the earth, for instance, or the human body, even its nervous
system. The psychologist's hypothetical predictions concerning the behaviour of the people of London, for
instance, have been proved utterly false. People, unfortunately, do not behave as the psychologists, presuming
omniscience, *feel* they should. The best time to subject
man to an "intelligence" test is perhaps at death. Then, it
may be asked, What did he do with the life God gave
him? The psychologist cannot forecast those results.
Having grown up at a time when humanism has enfiladed
nearly all thought and action with individualism, and
when psychology has sanctified man's faith in "intelligence", the emancipated intellectual feels little com-
punction to listen to the dictates of conscience. He feels
no need to refer to any authority other than his own
self-conscious intellect. Any idea so unscientific as an
"inner check" is a theme for derision. Cynically turning
away from first principles, he has placed his reliance solely
on the efforts of man and has failed to take into con-

sideration the possible consequences of divine intervention in the affairs of man. "You don't believe in God", said Hulme, "so you begin to believe that man is a god. You don't believe in Heaven, so you begin to believe in a heaven on earth."

In recent years the strange corollary of an expanding humanism has become a process of dehumanization.[1] What could be less Utopian than the hell in which the world finds itself today? We talk glibly of freedom and submit cheerfully to compulsion and constraint. We assume superiority in material possessions to find ourselves almost possessed by Aryan fiends. We have preached the religion of good-will and watched the antagonisms of the world increase. Toleration has bred intolerance. We have laughed with the "debunkers" to find ourselves "debunked" by dictators. Our zeal for clear-thinking has intensified suspicion, skepticism, and greed. Could anything be more heartless than an "economic" society ruled by a clique of intellectual aristocrats, inspired by class-hatred and prompted by a lust for power? Is this the communion of saints into which the communist would lead us after he has destroyed his twin the capitalist? Only a blind man dare say we have not lost the gleam. Only a foolish man would say we cannot find the grail. Only a coward will not venture in the quest. When we have laid aside the oppressive armour of self-sufficiency, our spirits will find space to breathe. When we have surmounted the degrading comfort of maginot-mindedness, we will find new courage in ourselves. Beyond the confines of this bank-

[1] This point of view is fully developed in Nicolas Berdyaev, *The Fate of Man in the Modern World*. Geoffrey Bles.

rupt humanism that reduces man to something less than "the paragon of animals", there lies a nobler humanism—a self purged of sordid indecencies, bright with sacrifice, and strong in faith. We need but the example of leadership and the discipline of personal decision.

When in the Great War the heavy artillery of the Huns was blowing to dust the sodden stones of Ypres, a new humanism was forged out of the iron in men's souls. When the blasted fields of the Somme were drenched with dreary misery, a new humanism was shaped by the common will for self-sacrifice. Sharing a common determination at Vimy Ridge inspired a brotherhood of service that few men, observing from afar the great moments of history, have ever experienced. Plunged in the quagmire of suffering that was Passchendaele, a new humanism was tempered by the sublimation of self in the devotion to duty and the common cause. Self became a means to an end; not something to be satisfied by reservations, but something to be realized through service. A serenity of spirit was born of high resolve and earnest discipline. The essential nobility and dignity of man were made manifest. Then came the "peace" to wreck this fellowship of self-surrendering knights.

The same sacrifice is possible in time of peace, but it takes more effort, more determination, and more devotion to a higher purpose. In war it is forced on man from without; in peace it springs from the spirit within. Hardly were the troops returned from the battlefields than the value of their experiences was discredited. No one knew where they had been or what they had done, and everyone had better keep away from them. The tall stories that some warriors in the base areas had to tell of their experiences were believed of all. Pensions, gratuities, reliefs were officially supplied, but war was reported to be a dirty business that was better forgotten. The war to end wars had been won, and the next order of business was the gratification of all the selfish appetites. While those who had lost sons and fathers in the conflict sat in mute wonderment, the shirkers came out of retirement to proclaim arrogantly that those who had served were the dupes of capitalism. If men would only be reasonable and listen to the intellectuals and believe in a league of nations and a league for peace and justice, the fear and hate, the greed and jealousy, the lust and ambition of which war is made, could, it was thought, be banished from the earth. This did not at the time seem a large order for the feeble intellect of man to undertake, but it was, while it lasted, a pleasant, if dangerous, fiction. Many veterans succumbed to the fashion of the time and fanned the flames of pacificism. So we sank back slack in body and in mind to take our ease in the self-satisfaction of the old humanism and dismissed the uneasiness of other less impressionable veterans and their loyal sympathizers as emotionalism and war-hysteria. The lessons of the war were too hard to learn.

Again today the patriotic youth of the land are rediscovering for us in the clouds and on the waves and by the shores the spirit of a new humanism. Their ideal of sacrifice puts to shame the selfish ambitions of petty political agitators and the nimble excuses of isolationists. Despite the defamation of conscience-stricken pacifists, these men have found a freedom in the high discipline of

service that they would not barter away for life itself.
Hear one of them:

> If this is where I get mine, up there where it is cold and clear,
> on a battlefield where the dead don't lie about and rot, where there
> is no mud and no stench, where there is moonlight by night and
> stars, and in the day the wizardry of intriguing cloud formations,
> and a blue sky above, where a man is free and on his own and the
> Devil and Jerry take the hindmost; if I get mine up there, there
> must be no regrets.
>
> I would have it that way. It is unfortunate that those of us
> who love life most, the very ones who so keenly seek to live the
> fullest life possible, must take the long chances that in so many
> cases cut it short. We are not blind to the odds against us; true,
> we laugh at them, or think lightly of them, but that is because we
> would have it no other way.
>
> I pity those who, living, live in fear of death.[1]

The writer of this testimony of unselfish youth has
passed beyond the reach of slander. His faith, the
psychologists may now in vain reduce to blind fanaticism,
but his character stands clear. When life on the plane of
action and life on the plane of imagination become one
and the same, a man may play the part of a hero in the
humble drama of his own life. Surely such devotion and
such sacrifice may be allowed to pass without drawing the
withering fire of cynicism from any quarter! Or have we
become at once so cruel and so cowardly that there is
nothing sacred left on earth? Have the little wonders of
the material world rendered us incapable of awe? Have
we become so callous in our self-sufficiency that we can
no longer find anything to revere? Perhaps our reforma-
tion is at hand!

[1] Fuller Patterson, R.C.A.F.

Whether we shall see the gleam this time and follow where it leads depends upon the breadth and depth of our crisis in the struggle and the length of its aftermath. Academic socialists will be as helpless as ourselves to make or break its intensity. If the vision splendid is vouchsafed to us, the old defunct humanism with its false values and mean standards will be discarded as an empty shell. A change will have taken place at the centre of man's being, and the futility of external material change will be obvious to all. Likewise will be revealed the folly of seeking freedom and "happiness" in geographical readjustment, economical realignment, and social reorganization on the basis of the old standards. So long as the old values prevail, it matters little whether the financial resources of the country are piled deep in one corner or spread thin over the whole field. What hope is there that money may be put where it will do the most good so long as covetous groups are warring for possession of the little that is left?

In the new humanism the philosophy of existence will take precedence over the philosophy of knowledge. Religious faith will be again the beginning of religious experience, and aesthetic, political, and social experience will assume importance relative to the destiny rather than the whim of man. For sake of clarity, the old humanism may be compared to an old-fashioned egg-beater, a conical spiral ascending through horizontal planes, and the new humanism to a wagon wheel, lying on its hub, with its axle eternally conjoining the earth with heaven, the finite with the infinite, the human with the divine. Whether the human passions of mankind fly outward toward the rim or inward toward the hub, the consequences will soon be evident in the varying tensions of divine faith, and grace, and love.

If it should be that we have reached the end of an era that began a thousand years ago and now draws to a close in a world at war, we may with some confidence look forward to finer things to come, for nothing could be much worse than the state from which we emerge.

Now we behold the amazing spectacle of states taking over the age-old claim of theocracy, that is, of totality, inevitably accompanied by suppression of free opinion. We again see people cutting each other's throats to support childish theories of how to produce paradise on earth. It is not very difficult to see that powers of the underworld—not to say of hell—which were formerly more or less successfully chained and made serviceable in a gigantic mental edifice, are now creating, or trying to create, a State slavery and a State prison devoid of any mental or spiritual charm. There are not a few people, nowadays, who are convinced that mere human reason is not entirely up to the enormous task of fettering the volcano.[1]

Unless man is to remain the victim of his own inventions, he must cure the disease of disbelief within himself. There is no escaping the jungle of chaos unless the material world is subjugated to the spiritual. Both are necessary to man's salvation, but it is the spirit that subdues and transforms matter to its purposes. The assumption of a reverse process distorts all values. Only through the spirit can we in truth discover our responsibility, obligation, and duty to God and to our fellow men; and this

[1] Carl Gustav Jung, *Psychology and Religion*. Yale University Press, 1938.

discovery is one of the products of personal faith and religious experience. The psychologist would set men apart; it is God who, when free from human restrictions, would draw men together. The intellect may provide the means to circumvent or to evade the will and the laws of God, but the calculating intellect can be as misleading and as foolhardy as the sympathetic intuition unless it, too, is responsible to a higher conscience. The brain-truster leaves God out of the picture because he cannot take Him into his dream.

Today, at last, the channels of life are deepening. As the current gathers head, the source, direction, and purpose of the flood appear less obscure. Compared with the apparent enormities of space, how infinitesimal is man's little knowledge and how limited his perspective! Viewed in the light of aeons that have come and gone and may be yet to come, how short is his little history! How absurd become his petty ambitions and conceits when cast against the background of eternal truth! Perhaps his only hope to give to life any lasting significance is by complete surrender to the will of God. How else but through the spirit can he find the strength to withstand the flood that would fling him outward to its farthest rim and the power that would draw him inward to life's core of faith. No matter how vast and incomprehensible the terrors of our punishment for this world's forgetfulness of God, redemption is a shallow hope unless the world's crisis becomes a personal crisis in each separate soul. Eventually must come life's zero hour!

I fled Him, down the nights and down the days;
 I fled Him, down the arches of the years;
I fled Him, down the labyrinthine ways
 Of my own mind; and in the mist of tears
I hid from Him, and under running laughter.
  Up vistaed hopes I sped;
  And shot, precipitated,
Adown Titanic glooms of chasmèd fears,
 From those strong Feet that followed, followed after.
  But with unhurrying chase,
  And unperturbèd pace,
Deliberate speed, majestic instancy,
  They beat—and a Voice beat
  More instant than the Feet—
'All things betray thee, who betrayest Me.'[1]

Political and social reformers, still clinging to the driftwood of shattered values, barely disturb the eddies at the current's edge. The main flood moves steadily on its way sublimely unaffected by any transfer of bullfrogs and waterlilies from one backwater to another. Abreast the main stream, however, are those who have surrendered self to the service of the nation. Only the quibbling intellectuals would question if these persons had become saints overnight, or wonder if the nation were truly aware of their doubtful sacrifice. Only isolationist professors, pacifist preachers, and socialist school teachers would question their sanity or seek to belittle their efforts by excusing their folly. The example of our warriors should be an inspiration to all compatriots because their serious act of self-denial, which puts to shame the self-righteousness of little moralists, is the beginning of the way that leads to supreme surrender. With the deepening of belief comes a new

[1] Francis Thompson, *The Hound of Heaven.* By permission of the publishers, Burns, Oates & Washbourne, Ltd.

sense of duty, and courage, and fortitude—the foundations of character, the fountain-head of culture. In a time, like the present, that tests men's souls, abiding loyalties are uncovered and tenable ideals are advanced. Not in the dictated theories of reformers, but in the will of a reformed people to live up to the highest principles of their faith within the laws of their belief, rests our hope of deliverance. Social reform is a result, not a cause, of belief, but some political zealots may be too stubborn and too impatient to deny themselves a splurge of revolution or of plunder.

Perhaps it will take a major national calamity to reveal to some people the hollowness of false gods. It is hoped, however, that humanity will find its way out before the communist has appeased his greed and the anarchist has expressed his will. War is bad enough, but it is by no means the worst disaster that can befall us. What if the heritage bequeathed to us in trust should in our time be lost through lack of care or courage! France, self-secure, forgot her faith. She permitted theories to supplant belief, and speculation to usurp the throne of truth. Bleeding in the chains of humiliation, she is now trying to find her soul. Is this to be our fate? Is our survival to be contingent to the theorists' gratification of their lust for power, their class-hatred, and their betrayal of youth. Surely we are not going to be deluded by hypothetical speculations on the nature of a post-war world! Canadians are surely not fighting for a state of such Utopian perfection as, by the very nature of creation, is impossible of achievement, a state in which cranks will cease from troubling and agitators will be at rest. Some of these theorists are doubtless sincere. They probably believe with child-like earnestness that justice is a product of easy manipulation; but what they seek can never be achieved on the basis of the old humanistic values. Not only are they standing unwittingly in their own light, but they are deceiving youth with all its generous capacity for faith and courage and sacrifice. From this, springs the pathos of the drama of existence. The disease of mankind is too deep-seated to be reached by superficial tonics. The complexion of the post-war world will reflect what we learn from our experiences in a world at war. When we have passed through the Valley of the Shadow of Death we may find the Way of the Cross. It is the hard way, but there is no other way to social justice, or to any other justice.

It is said, for instance, by those who still hug the security and comfort of an overweening complacency or isolationism that their education and training are responsible for their attitude and condition. This is a poor excuse, however, for their continued desire to play safe and selfish. During the Great War some people deliberately side-stepped their responsibility and misused the trust reposed in them. Since the last war a whole system of education has been built up on this continent in support of the position of the isolationist and those who consider self-interest first to be served. Up to the outbreak of the war in 1939 the so-called "progressive" education, which is based solidly in the old self-centred humanism, was regarded by educational engineers and socialist teachers as the hope of the world, and it spread rapidly everywhere with devastating effect on the character and the culture of the people. But this "progressive" education, that would *dare to build a new social order,* had failed to take into account the emergency of war and the numerous other exigencies that beset us in a very real world. The thunder of the guns has exploded the balloon. The modern isolationist is at once the cause and the effect of the hopeless condition he laments. He is unhappy because his appetites and desires are unsatisfied. The cult of *self* has deprived him of the ritual of living. He lives at the rim, the outer fringe, not the hub, the heart, the core of human experience. He has not surrendered to the leadership of the soul, but rather has capitulated to the tyranny of his senses. In a wilderness of apparently chaotic forces he cries aloud for security which, like a mirage, fades before his narrow earth-bound vision. Lacking the essential faith and sincerity of a controlled, integrated, and determined character, he can never, without making a complete about-turn, achieve serenity. Like a shell-shocked mule, his Life-in-Death existence is intolerable. He is demoralized by the hollowness of the material world and the vanity of believing in progress as a series of advancing evolutionary changes. The old-fashioned egg-beater has collapsed, and he is helplessly entangled in its strands. The wrath of God may be one proof of His love.

The optimist, however, is unprepared to meet the challenge of this world's inhumanity. His blind but vain belief in himself and his sentimental philosophy of brotherly love has so warped his understanding of man that he is now shocked to see what he before resolutely refused to believe. The chaos that confronts him, when his man-made world suddenly collapses, buries beneath it all his hopes and discloses indescribable spectres. Where

there is no fear of God, the mind resounds to the tread of
fears invented and perhaps more terrible! Compared
with the optimist's despair, the pessimism of the Christian,
who recognizes the double nature in man, affords a
cheerful prospect and a hope. When the flimsy structure
of materialism begins to tremble, the Christian has still
beneath him and around him the firm foundations of a
faith that is larger than the mean confines of self and
more enduring than the products of scientific progress or
evolution. By what he contemplates, the Christian is
neither deluded nor completely discouraged. His position
is never utterly hopeless, but the challenge of his creed
is all-embracing and uncompromising. It puts to shame
the colourful but wasteful practices of optimistic
adventurers in secular socialism, because it goes to the heart
of the problem of man's imperfect state.

The quibbler, of course, will raise the cry of extremes—
Would not a narrow ecclesiastical culture be far worse than
a broad secular culture? There need be no fear of such
a transformation suddenly taking place! The millenium
is not yet quite at hand! A nation of quickened spirits may
be a sign of the times, but surely not the consummation of
a communion of saints! Browning reminds us, however,

> Let us not always say
> 'Spite of this flesh today
> I strove, made head, gained ground upon the Whole!'
> As the bird wings and sings,
> Let us cry, 'All good things
> Are ours, nor soul helps flesh more now
> Than flesh helps soul.'[1]

[1] *Rabbi Ben Ezra.*

The material and the spiritual, the body and the soul, are necessary to each other. The external and the internal worlds are counterparts and need each other. Today there is a deepening of belief, the spirit of a new seriousness is abroad in the world. With this deepening of purpose comes a revelation of the inadequacy of "progressivism" in education and with it the imperative need for something more closely related to the nature of man's destiny and existence. We may be on the threshold of a new renaissance.

The following observations of Walter Lippmann emphasize the inadequacy of false standards:

> Man can bear anything except a sense of his own utter demoralization. As long as he has the support of a discipline which is rational and transcends his immediate promptings, he will endure discomfort, pain and danger. That is why men with faith can face martyrdom while men without it feel stricken when they are not invited to dinner. . . . The secular man—the man who obeys his impulses and knows no reason that transcends his wishes—this secular man, now dominant in the world, has for his chief article of faith an ideal of secular progress which is totally alienated from and profoundly opposed to the real character of the human person. . . . For in the secular tradition men are not taught to think that the disciplining of their desires to a rational measure is indispensable if they are ever to be truly satisfied. Thus the modern conception of progress is self-defeating. For it is based on a fundamental misunderstanding of the economy of human existence.[1]

Progressive education is just what its name implies, a desire to keep abreast of the changing material world. Its very existence depends on the spread and the spreading of wealth and privileges on the basis of outworn values. It

[1] "Man's Image of Man", an address to the American Catholic Philosophical Association, 1941.

is founded on the false assumption that freedom is a purchasable commodity, an endowment that can be *granted* the pupil. It would, perhaps, be nearer the truth to assume that freedom is a priceless condition that may be *attained* through the persistent effort, self-control, and responsible action of men of character. It aims at the elimination of everything that may impede the free development of "personality" through an artificially stimulated self-expression. The "personality" it would develop is an attractive mask, an alluring show-window, to hide the restlessness, the tawdriness, within. On superficial social levels it can be both serviceable and successful, but on its highest level, it produces, not leaders, but committee-room quibblers. In all departments of life progressivism has left its mark. The half-truths of the cynic, the skeptic, and the "debunker", provide the timely novelty and smartness that the fleeting mind requires to relieve the possible tension that a crisis in the inner man may provoke. These clowns perform a very useful function in life—we should fare poorly without them—but when their comedy is taken seriously, all values are upset. Loyalty to Christ and allegiance to the King become less significant than glib slogans and brilliant witticisms. Criticize the impressive masks of these merry tragedians, and both the intellectual humanists, who mistake their cunning for wisdom, and the emotional humanists, who gloat over the defeatist despair they engender, will charge you with lack of charity and good will.

There was a time when a man's word was as good as his bond, and the principle of his actions sprang from firmly held beliefs. The ten commandments once formed an acceptable code for conduct, not a stimulating challenge to the evasive schemes of the nimble and arrogant intellect of man. Today the so-called "ideal" man, confronted by a problem, proceeds to intellectualize the facts. The process of these cogitations, or relative "interpretations", he dignifies by the name of reasoning. It is quick and subtle, but its chief faith resides in its own self-conscious flight. So earnest and meticulous in its search for truth, it flees the very object that it seeks. It is like an airplane aloft without a base. "Now, let me see; what are the facts?" and "Well, I'll have to give some consideration to that point." These expressions are typical, fluttering signals of distress, mere excuses for the inability to make decisions. When these gyrations reach their climax, the reasoning, by implication, runs as follows:

Hitler despises the intellectuals.
Hitler is wrong.
Therefore, the intellectuals are right.

Hitler has laid stress on the development of character.
Hitler is wrong.
Therefore, it is wrong to lay stress on the development of character.

A man can hardly come to grips with the problems of life and master them by the use of this sort of logic. Even the best strategy will not save from defeat an army that has lost the will to fight. War has evoked a new seriousness, but what may become of this attitude depends to some extent on our ability to rid ourselves of a lot of mistaken notions about education.

Why should English society continue to cohere? The answer is so simple in form and so religious in expression that to some it may appear mere evasion, to others mere unction. It is: 'For the making of souls.' One recalls Keats' comment repudiating the idea that this world is a vale of tears and insisting that it is 'a vale of soul-making.' Many things, including some suffering, are necessary to that process, but it is the end for which society and all its functions exist.

How does society cohere? . . . Perhaps the answer is that there can be no answer in set terms, so deep do the forces lie. But if we may venture a tentative answer in terms so simple and platitudinous that they seem absurd, we would say 'By faith and love.' The terms look empty enough until they receive their proper content. No definition or social science or system of law can confer that content. It can be given only by life and sound education and the grace of God.

It may be, then, that the most essentially religious thing in us is that by virtue of which we cohere as a society, and that here is the heart of education's business.[1]

When such beliefs are more generally held, Christian art, the handmaiden of Christian religion, will again be a creative influence in the life and work of man. It is time, then, to shift the emphasis in education from the narrow basis of intellectualism to the broad foundations of creative living, from extensive knowledge to intensive experience. The years that lie before us, whether they be spent in peace or war, are likely to be rough and strenuous. As individuals and as a nation we shall need all the courage, fortitude, and tenacity of purpose with which our pioneer forefathers were endowed. If we are not to go down to ignominious defeat, our spirits will require food more nourishing than flimsy theories and speculations. If, as a people, we hope to be worthy of our heritage, we should shift the emphasis in education, as in religion and state-

[1] F. Clarke, *Education and Social Change*. Sheldon Press.

craft, from the Utopian concept of a world civilization devoid of religious and political differences, to the ever present concept of the individual human soul with its spiritual as well as material needs and its infinite possibilities. It is time to view the problem of human existence from the top and not from the bottom, from the centre rather than from the circumference. "For what is a man profited, if he shall gain the whole world, and lose his own soul?" In the exigencies of life and the inevitability of death the tenets of progressivism are rendered obsolete.

EDUCATION

When God, not man, is acknowledged to be the centre of the universe, emphasis falls on absolute spiritual values rather than on relative material trivialities. When recognition is given to the fact that a human being is essentially a spiritual creature, less attention is given to "conditioned environments" and "world cultures". Place first things first, and the rest will follow; place first things in a secondary position and what follows will be characterized by what someone has described as "change, more change, and then mere change". It is not that less attention should be concentrated on the immanence of God, but more faith centred in the transcendent God. "Now faith is the substance of things hoped for, the evidence of things not seen."

Despite all the conundrums that man has been given the power to solve, despite this "brave new world" that he has made for himself to live in, the solution of the problem that confronts his soul remains unchanged. Any educational engineer or philosopher of education who fails to take into account this primary fundamental problem, is only an administrator of personnel. No matter how efficient are the defensive disciplines he recommends, how broad or narrow the curricula he proposes, or how novel the methods he advocates, he provides only different avenues for self-deception and social confusion. Any educational system that is not at least pointed in the direction of this problem and its possible personal solution for every member, fails to "recognize that the spiritual powers are the noblest and most important of our nature." Quibblers will see in this only a stuffy asceticism; it is, on the contrary, only through the spirit that man can attain the genuine freedom of which he dreams.

If the purpose of education, in both the arts and the sciences, is to inspire man to live courageously and train him to live creatively, it must be informed by a dynamic spiritual energy that comes from the one source of all spiritual life—from God. Without it education remains materialistic, self-centred, and self-consuming; and the training of pupils is modelled on the manufacture of shafts and gears. But if the aim of education is centripetal in the sense that body, mind, and soul are one, instead of centrifugal in the sense that body, mind, and soul are separate entities, the emphasis will fall on the discovery of principles rather than on the acquisition of facts, on the development of character rather than the sharpening of wits, on the shaping of the will rather than the awakening of desires. Education will aim to emphasize the invisible unity of all life in the spirit, rather than the visible diversity of man's material environment and his sophisticated life.

In education that is truly Christian, the fostering of an attitude of predilection is inherent. The materials of education are given different values according to the quality of the experiences they afford and the priority significance they command in the life of man. How different is this from the cultivation of an attitude of superficial toleration of everything, and the worship of the fetish of equality in order to achieve mediocrity? Height and depth, rather than length and breadth, are the more significant dimensions in education. Life that could be rendered free and creative through intensive experience, should not be exhausted by the measurable burden of extensive knowledge. Shift the emphasis from the learning of facts to the development of insight into their relationship, from the encouragement of self-expression to the initiation of creative power, and education will produce fewer "honest intellectuals" and more "nobodies who maintain the state of the world by their unchronicled worth". Shift the emphasis from the gathering of opinions to the making of decisions, from contemplation to forthgoing, from calculation to spontaneity, from formal analysis to integrated synthesis and education will produce less pomposity, spurious efficiency, and puerile officiousness, but more genuine leadership. Shift the emphasis from external illusions to internal truth, from satisfaction in a material connection with the things of the spirit to ardour for a personal encounter with the spirit, and education will find the perspective and meaning of a crusade. It will no longer be an end in itself, but a means to an end. Fewer people will think only of their privileges and more people will be ready to fulfil their obligations.

If education is to play its part in the regeneration of
the individual, it must enthrone an ideal nobler than the
service of self. Surely this can not be achieved by
liberating the predatory instincts of ten million selfish
spites or by creating what the Archbishop of York recently
called a "welter of competing selfishnesses"! Education
must think less of social amenities and candle-lit culture
and more of solving the problems of living. In a world
of cruel extremes, of life and death, of peace and war, of
joy and sorrow, of success and failure, of good and evil,
education should provide not an escape from the storm,
but a crusade into it and through it. It should turn the
self instinct to nobler uses than its own satisfaction. Much
of the evil that is concocted in the heart of man is the
product of his boredom with the mean and narrow confines of self-sufficiency. Education should help man to get
outside himself the better to see within. It should provide
training in the fine art of self-realization through
sublimation. It should reveal the way of the spirit that
leads to all the great freedoms. It should concentrate less
attention on how to make a living and more on how to
live, less on how to succeed and more on how to pray. It
should think less of policy and more of principle, less of
intellect and more of spirit, less of respectability and more
of decency. It should proclaim less for personal rights
and more for reasonableness. Part of the job of education
is to quicken the spirit and keep the faith.

"We must bring God back into government; we must
bring God back into education; we must bring God back
into economic life; we must bring God back, indeed, into
all life, private and public, individual and social." Thus

reads a manifesto by sixteen prelates of the Catholic
Church in the United States. The first step in carrying
out such a proclamation is to remove all the human bar-
riers, restrictions, and limitations that man has placed
upon the freedom of God. This can be achieved only by
regenerated individuals obedient to the authority and will
of God. It is only through the individual that the
beneficence of divine grace can spread to society. "My
only hope for the world" wrote Gladstone, "is the bringing
of the human mind into contact with Divine Revelation."
Man, without God, is helpless. His best effort, despite all
his devilish cunning, is unworthy of him and his real
potentialities—the disciplined use of the gifts that God
has bestowed upon him. Discarding these spiritual gifts
as worthless, man may now be on the verge of discovering
to his sorrow that there is nothing else of worth in a
material world.

The violent eruptions that now shake the mental super-
structure of the world are as much the result of spiritual as
of economic or political collapse. It is understatement to
dismiss them as examples of social unrest, and this would
be humorous were it not so serious. When men and
nations have rediscovered a deeper faith in God, their
attitude to one another may improve. In all departments
of life we have produced some clever, skilful, and efficient
technicians, but we have among us few men of significant
character and profound belief. We have only ourselves to
blame for our misfortunes if we have lost the faith of our
forefathers. If Christ is the true mediator and arbiter
between man and man in a Christian country, the brotherhood of man in Christ may some day be achieved. But in

the words of a great saint, we must "work as if everything depended upon us; pray as if everything depended upon God". Our success may be small, but it will be greater than would be the efforts of those who can take nothing on faith. A "new" society cannot be built by individuals "whose hearts are still filled with dark and confused desires". The responsibility for the regeneration of a people rests not on the priest or the pastor but on ourselves; not primarily on the state, or the church, or the school, but on each one of us as individuals. "Christian example will change the lives of people better than anything else." Our job is to translate belief into action.

Let no man despise thy Youth; but be thou an example of the believers, in word, in conversation, in charity, in spirit, in faith, in purity. Till I come, give attendance to reading, to exhortation, to doctrine. Neglect not the gift that is in thee, which was given thee by prophecy, with the laying on of the hands of the presbytery. Meditate on these things; give thyself wholly to them; that thy profiting may appear to all. Take heed unto thyself, and unto the doctrine; continue in them; for in doing this thou shalt both save thyself, and them that hear thee.[1]

This instruction is clear, but its challenge will never be taken up while men are content to quibble about doctrine and dogma and to intellectualize on Original Sin and the transference of guilt. The irony of fate may be their forced acceptance of foreign doctrines and codes about which their own rationalizations will be the bitterest gall.

Beneath the rubble of a false humanism there lies the spirit of a true philosophy of life. Behind this tyranny of self-interest there resides, ready to be awakened, a nobler self capable of great sacrifice. Even the vacuum created

---

[1] Timothy, 4: 12-16.

by the exclusive intellectuals may yet become a receptacle
for spiritual faith. Within the very church which seemed
to be degenerating rapidly into a social club for the discussion of anything under the sun, there still stands the
altar of divine truth. The school which yesterday was
devoting attention to "exploratory" programmes for the
glorification of irresponsible self-expression may yet
become the builder of responsible men and women. "It
was always through enfeeblement of character", said
Gustave Le Bon, "and not through enfeeblement of
intelligence, that the great peoples disappeared from
history." In the midst of material chaos we may yet find
the Cross and with it the spiritual faith that can make us
worthy of our heritage and our destiny, worthy of the
sacrifices that have been and are being made for us, and
worthy of membership in the commonwealth of nations
that must one day assume the leadership of an exhausted
and broken-hearted world. It may be that in the centuries
immediately before mankind—recent advances in science
already consolidated, and creative art again a source of
inspiration—it may be that new revelations in the realm
of the spirit may be the next gift of grace vouchsafed to
all the faithful.

POETRY

The flying wheel of the world's circumstance is never
still. Along its spokes run the opposing forces that seek
and flee the centre, and between them the restless heart of
man today, as yesterday, shifts to and fro. The ancients
moved along one spoke; we move along another. Some-

times the swing is outward to material progress; sometimes it is inward to spiritual serenity.

There is a spiritual kind of nourishment supplied by religion, art, philosophy, and literature, not less important for the well-being of mankind than food and shelter. When it is absent, man rapidly goes back to the dirt from which he sprung. . . . Like philosophy it bakes no bread, but it can give God, Freedom, and Immortality.

The major poets and inspired thinkers of each generation, peering into the throbbing heart of experience, seeking the pivot of existence, face inward from the wheel's circumference. Whether the poet is enthralled by his own spiritual ecstasy, or mental processes, or physical sensations, he tries to bring what he feels into harmony with the invisible pulsations sounding through the universe. In various ways he seeks to define the delicate relationship of man to man, to nature, and to God. Hoping to find the reality that underlies appearances, he seeks the centre of the flying wheel.

The ways of the Spirit no man knows; but it is manifest that for the opening mind, whether of youth or of older years, the sense of eternity, however delicate, subtle, and silent is its realm, is fed nobly, sweetly, and happily, in those poets in whom the spirit of man crying for expression unlocks the secrecy of its relations to the infinite.

There, whosoever will, shall open the book of all the world, and read and ponder, and shall enter the common mind of man which is there contained, and avail of its wisdom and absorb its energies into his own and become one with it in insight, power, and hope, and ere he is aware shall find himself mingling with the wisest, the holiest, the loveliest, as their comrade and peer. He shall have poet and sage to sup with him, and their meal shall be the bread of life.[1]

[1] George E. Woodberry, *The Torch*. Harcourt Brace.

George Russell (A.E.) once said, "But the good things of God, in the natural order, are free for everybody. *The uncovering of these free values is the working of the real poets,* and when carried on in connection with the re-establishment of a rural culture, cannot be without deep social significance." These words of an Irish poet and seer were addressed to a people of very special temperament in a country-side unlike our own, but they are more likely to reflect a truth than are the words of those critics and evaluators who proclaim that England has been without a poet since John Donne, or had not had one until T. S. Eliot came upon the scene. It is typical of literary academicians to "school" poets, analyze periods, and intel-lectualize about movements, forgetting that the poet's chief duty, as Spingarn has said, "is to be true to his art, and to express his vision of reality as well as he can."[1]

Suddenly comes the realization that types of personality are eternal, and that whatever age they live in, these types will produce the same kind of poetry, however different it may be in degree. The creative, character-making type will produce now a Chaucer, now a Shakespeare, now a Browning; the conscious artist is now a Pope, now a Rossetti, now a Housman; the solitary mystic appears as a Vaughan, as a Blake, as an Emily Brontë; the sophisticated man of the world writes in one age as a Dryden, in another as a Byron; the intellectual takes one incarnation in a Donne and another in a Shelley and another in an Eliot; the great struggle between the Puritan and the Epicurean fights itself out in one age in the splendour of a Milton, in another in the unhappiness of an Arnold.[2]

The time is surely past when the critic or the teacher can afford to be only a formalist, a moralist, a melodist,

[1] J. E. Spingarn, *Creative Criticism.* Oxford, 1931.
[2] Elizabeth Drew, *Discovering Poetry.* Norton, 1933.

an imagist, an emotionalist or an intellectualist, seeking in a poem only the reflection of his personal whim. What really matters is the degree, the quality of the poetic experience latent in the work of art. What did the poet perceive, and how successful was his effort to preserve his vision and make it accessible to others?

Pause for a moment and consider what it is we in truth desire, of what we are in search. Nothing else, surely than a reconciliation between ourselves and the world to which we belong, that is—may we not say?—an attunement or concord between Being and Becoming, which if attainable were pure felicity, a reconciliation or harmony which human wisdom and experience fail in the world they so anxiously contemplate either to perceive or to effect. Yet since in the arts they are in a manner found together, in essence one, for this reason human nature derives from the arts its deepest satisfactions. Poetry appears to be something we have always known in our hearts, but have never before had so vividly presented to us. In these arts of divination the waking consults the dreaming mind; the surface consciousness, in search of more favourable omens, enquires of the oracle, of the better informed and wiser soul. And the inspired priestess by whom the world is seen in the wider perspective answers, "Your experience is real, but consult the God within you and know that this real is not the whole of reality."[1]

It may be the poets who see the light of life. It was once said that "Shelley for all his faults was nearer to Christ—more saintly—than many of the wasteful clergy of his time." It may be that the inspired poets, whose master-pieces are like flagstones in the path to God, may yet, by reawakening belief in the intuitive guidance of great art, teach us how to recover our faith and how to find attune-

[1] W. Macneile Dixon, *The Human Situation* (being the Gifford Lectures delivered in the University of Glasgow, 1935-37). E. Arnold, 1938.

ment between Being and Becoming. It is the poet who is *of* mankind, but who is sufficiently aloof *from* mankind that he can speak *for* mankind. He speaks for the whole of man, his intuition as well as his reason. It may be that the poet can yet help man to find himself and his real potentialities in higher and deeper planes of experience. In his own peculiar way the poet can draw man into the silence of reflection for the replenishment of his strength, can help him to justify himself to himself so that he can live with himself, can teach him how to transcend his own selfishness.

These are the features and faculties in man that the poets love and admire, his endurance, his resolution, his heroisms, his quixotry. Yes, the quixotry, the inexplicable preference, even to his own hurt, for the noble and magnanimous, the high and honourable things. Miracles they are that outmiracle all others, if atoms and the void produced these human qualities. It is in the exalted thoughts and still more soaring dreams of 'that wild swan the soul', the admirable lunacies, the sudden gleams that illuminate the sombre landscape of human life that the poets find the revelation of the vital truth. They issue no commandments, they censure not, they upbraid not. In the fierce turmoil they are not utterly discouraged. They sympathize with every creature. They know, and yet, *mirabile dictu*, love the world. Theirs is a postulate, if you like, yet a postulate we must all make, if we are to enter the region of meanings at all, that our natural capacities, our natural instincts are not the casual spindrift of time, but of an earlier birth and longer lineage. As in the darkness, in the organism not yet born, the eye is formed to correspond to things invisible, and thus with confidence anticipates a world to come, so the soul's faculties, for love, for joy, for admiration, for achievement, correspond to a reality which exists, and is by them foretold. The soul does not provide itself with a passport for an imaginary country, and cannot vibrate to a note unsounded in the universe.[1]

[1] W. Macneile Dixon, *The Human Situation*.

It is the inspired poets who sound the note and point the way. Along with other supreme artists, they have kept the faith that inspired mediaeval art, the faith the the ego-centric philosophers may have lost. Fortunately their art, although it may not always be so immediate in its appeal as is the art of the composer or the painter, nevertheless encompasses a wider and more easily accessible range of human experience than do the other arts. But no matter how competent the artist, he is like Andrea del Sarto, powerless without the gift of inspiration to speak significantly *for* mankind. There are poets and poetasters; and mere artistic competence is no guarantee of inspiration.

Something is certainly happening to English painting; something not unworthy to be compared with what is happening to English literature. Each of them is ceasing to rely on its amusement-value to an audience of wealthy philistines, and is substituting for that aim not one of amusement-value to an audience of wage-earners or dole-drawers, nor yet one of magical value, but one of genuine artistic competence. But the question is whether this ideal of artistic competence is directed backwards into the alley of nineteenth-century individualism, where the artist's only purpose was to express "himself", or forwards into a new path where the artist, laying aside his individualistic pretensions, walks as the spokesman of his audience.[1]

In recent years one section of English poetry has become stuffy with intellectualism. It is remarkable chiefly for its novelty and its self-assertion. It clamours to be heard; it makes little effort to be understood. Its glory is its self-sufficiency. When it forgets itself, it rises momentarily to poignancy. It believes, according to the following opinion, that it has a mission:

[1] R. G. Collingwood, *The Principles of Art*. Clarendon, 1938.

The complete revolutionary writer will introduce a new morality into literature. Most great literature has a coherent philosophy at the back of it: to English literature, from the mystery plays to Wordsworth, the Christian philosophy has been a background—and often the backbone too. But for the last 100 years this background has been disintegrating, till now nothing remains of it but a few faded tatters stitched together with every variety of pseudo-scientific, mystico-emotional, liberal-humanist material. In contrast with this, the work of a revolutionary writer backed by a thoroughly assimilated dialectical materialism is bound to be impressive.[1]

The attempt "to explain life from below upwards instead of from above downwards" is the mistake of all the anthropocentric humanists. "The *Fine Arts,* however, and the art of the poet itself," writes Maritain,[2] "being ordered to a transcendental world, are specially designed by nature to bring it into our midst." And again he explains:

But what Wilde, choked by the paper roses of aestheticism, failed to understand is that our art does not derive from itself alone what it imparts to things; it spreads over them a secret which it first discovered in them, in their invisible substance or in their endless exchanges and correspondences. Take it out of "that blessed reality given once for all, in the centre of which we are situated" and it ceases to be. It transforms, removes, brings closer together, transfigures; it does not create. It is by the way in which he changes the shape of the universe passing through his mind, in order to make a form apprehended in things shine upon a matter, that the artist impresses his signature upon his work. He recomposes for each, *according as the poetry in him changes him*, a world more real than the reality offered to the senses.[2]

It may be that through intensive poetic experience we can achieve a humility that is the beginning of faith, and

[1] C. Day Lewis, *Revolution in Writing*. Hogarth, 1935.
[2] Jacques Maritain, *Art and Scholasticism*. Sheed & Ward, 1930.

can perceive that personal sacrifice is the supreme ecstasy. It is inspired poetry that can provide a means for our forth-going, can help to sustain us in the turbulent stream of life, can stimulate creative thought, and can exhilarate us with "a sense of increased capacity."

From its earliest recorded beginnings in Caedmon, English literature has been in large part, and sometimes perhaps by accident, a receptacle of Christian faith and points of view. Although neither priests nor theologians, the poets often view the same horizons as the religious mystics see. The poets have their own special way of looking at life. They often strike the posture and profess the meaning of our deepest needs. Into the art of repre-sentation and of sense-appeal, they have a power to breathe a spirit that gives art character. There are some things, moreover, that can be crystallized in poetry better than they can be in any other art. Literary masterpieces, al-though in no sense religious documents, are often endowed with a spiritual unity, insight, and exaltation which quicken the spirit of the reader to behold. Great poetry is a body charged with spiritual energy for those who can lay hold upon it.

English poetry, properly taught as an art for the sake of experience, is one of the finest of all educational instru-ments, and may in its effect reach deeply into the life of a people and help them to discover their traditions, their character, and their destiny. Among the chief responsi-bilities of the school are the cultivation of loyalties and sympathies, the inspiration of courage and fortitude, the inculcation of honesty and integrity, and the deepening of the insight and the tempering of the will. Heart and brain must be trained to work together and through each other. "The mind working alone without the heart can of itself never arrive at any conclusions regarding human problems which really touch the vital issues involved."[1]

On the teacher of English *in the teaching of his subject* falls a fair share of the weight of these responsibilities, but he must *teach* and not preach or proselytize. His desk makes a poor soap-box and a worse pulpit. His job is not to make converts or to claim disciples, but to bring his subject "contagiously alive". If he is a Christian and a patriot, his pupils will learn from his example all that both he and they can understand and appreciate in our way of life. If he is an atheist with a socialist's zeal for conditional patriotism, his pupils will become the dupes of the first demagogue who comes their way. If he is a good teacher and a scholar, his loyalty to his subject and his passion for its teaching will carry him over the pitfalls of intellectualism that reduces literature to propaganda, checks rather than corrects the powers of intuition, discounts mysticism and inspiration, and distorts the arts by twisting them to the shape of self. It is not enough that the teacher should be industrious, efficient, and honest; he must lay claim to a faith that passes beyond the farthest reaches of the calculating intellect. The responsibility of the teacher is made quite clear by the Hadow Report, which states: "The teaching of religious knowledge, like that of English, cannot be confined to a separate period or number of periods. It will affect the teaching of other

[1] Lawrence Hyde, *The Learned Knife*. Howe.

subjects, such as history and literature, and the wise teacher will be anxious, in the various departments of school activity, to bring home to the pupils, as far as their capacity allows, the fundamental truths of religion and their bearing on human life and thought." It is not enough to ask a clergyman to visit the school or to ask the pupils to pay daily lip-service to The Lord's Prayer. The initiative must be taken by the teacher *in his teaching*. The responsibility of the teacher of English is to bring into the experience of the pupil, as far as possible, the fundamental truths of the real experiencers, the inspired poets and thinkers who have left in their works the permanent records of the crises, great and small, in their own existences. But he errs sadly if he aims, with the curriculum, at the reading of *more* poetry, rather than at more *reading* of poetry.

In a rapidly changing age, there is a real danger that being well informed may prove incompatible with being cultivated. To be well informed, one must read quickly a great number of merely instructive books. To be cultivated, one must read slowly and with a lingering appreciation the comparatively few books that have been written by men who lived, thought and felt with style.[1]

If the teaching of poetry is a creative process in a system of creative education, the materials of study and the basis of selection are important. If the poetry in our school anthologies is selected to illustrate a chronological order, literary movements, artistic forms, exotic symbols, beautiful images, competent craftsmanship, or to set a new standard in amusement value, how small is our hope of perceiving the attitudes of the great experiencers of love, hope, despair, loneliness, friendship, courage, misery,

[1] Aldous Huxley, *Texts and Pretexts.*

sacrifice, serenity, humour, hypocrisy, gratitude, liberty, generosity, etc.! An anthology of poetry for our schools should present a core of significant poetic experience, properly graded, and centred on our fundamental problems. "It is the peaks of human experience which are significant for us, not the valleys."[1]

The teacher, however, is perhaps the most important single unit in the whole educational system. He stands in the front line of educational philosophy, administration, and practice; the success or the failure of the system is largely in his keeping. It is to be hoped that the time will come when he is not kept so busy that he has no time to think; unless thinking is to be a privilege reserved for the professional educational theorists. The judicious introduction of a little "teacher freedom" at this point in the system might improve the theory as well as the practice in education and this in turn might result in benefits to the pupils and the nation. The lawyer, for instance, who is kept too busy with cases, soon finds his sense of jurisprudence dulled. The teacher, too, like the artist, needs a time for reflection—periodical withdrawals into silence for the refreshment of his spirit and the replenishment of his power. The real teacher is interesting because he is interested. His power to interest others in experiences that are worthy of their efforts to apprehend is far more important than their power to find an interest in things that they like. Neither his enjoyment, nor their enjoyment, but rather his imaginative insight into the significance of his subject, is his driving force, perhaps the secret of his devotion to his task. He is the incarnation of all that he

---

[1] *The Learned Knife.*

professes, and his sound scholarship should be a guarantee that he would not, for the sake of political, educational, or social expediency, flatter the emerging *self* of the pupil out of all proportion to the pupil's capacity to understand.

In a recent book of fiction, one character, a Mr. Freneau, a teacher of music in a progressive college for young ladies, explains his position to his dean in the following words:

> For the playing of Bach, for the playing of all the old music, one needs unselfishness. The performer must not be the center of any attention. He interprets only. He is the medium through which music flows. Never can he allow himself to get in the way. But this new music, Mademoiselle, is selfish music. The performer is the center. He gets in the way. He improvises. The composer— he is nothing. The performer takes his theme and does what he likes with it. That is the modern method, Mademoiselle. But if one has learned to be unselfish in the old music, one lacks the ego to play the new. When these moderns look at any piece of music, they think only of how they can change it. They make it all— personal. No, Mademoiselle, I cannot train my pupils, by means of the old, to be successful in the new. In the old music, one lost one's self. In the new, one exhibits one's self.[1]

For the teacher of English the meaning of this passage is clear. By analogy it suggests the nature of materials and of methods in English. By implication it gives the reasons for both. In our schools today boys and girls are looking for those ideas and ideals that give substance and meaning to life. They are bewildered by the arrogance of the new story. They instinctively prefer the old faith that carries "the funded meaning of the past into the experiences of the present". They understand best its images, its feelings, its metaphors, and its challenge. Their capacity for sacri-

[1] Dorothy Walworth, *Feast of Reason*. Farrar & Rinehart, 1941.

fice is enormous. Their industry and endurance are immeasurable. Their resilience is as refreshing as it is swift. Today their elder brothers are bearing the sins of us all on their shoulders. They want and deserve something better than a false humanistic philosophy can offer them with its emphasis on materialism, naturalism, and the transitory joys of appetite. Unless they are to grow up to be hollow men they must be shown the way to life's higher values—the way of the great experiencers who have had the power to see and to hear the significant things and the gift to speak significantly for the rest of mankind.

Our way of life is paved with the practice of Christian principles. To ask our pupils, passing along it, to recognize the rights of others for human reasons only, is dangerous, because they learn thus to secrete their thoughts, feelings, and perhaps their instincts, but not to sublimate them and render them constructively useful in society. They soon learn to pass along, with their prejudices, on the other side, and it is absurd to call their cheerful indifference to their responsibilities goodwill. As teachers of English our job is simply this: to help the pupil to achieve, by the exercise of his own creative faculties, an experience somewhat similar to that of the inspired poet. The boys and girls in our secondary schools are quick to respond to such leadership when it speaks with the conviction of experience. The world stands in desperate need of it today. It has grown weary of compromise, procrastination, and expediency; it suspects what it understands of the endlessly relative programmes of the wily socialist. It seeks a new set of presuppositions in which the spirit of Christianity is the keystone. Our job is to teach by precept and example, even as the poets, the real experiencers, do, for the spiritual regeneration of mankind. To try to save the privileges of our free way of life by any other means, in either peace or war, is simply futile. This is the way to our salvation both as individuals and as members of the commonwealth of English-speaking peoples. It may also be eventually the way of all mankind caught in the tensions and the conflicts of the flying wheel of this world's circumstance.

> No star is ever lost we once have seen,
> We always may be what we might have been.

Chapter Two
EXPERIENCING POETRY

THE aims of literary study are as many and various as the people who propose them. Such a statement as this is not without its appeal, and champions of personal liberty hail it as the first banner in their cause. Let every man carry his own standard, be his principles and purposes what they may! Poetry may be the highest form of the literary art, but values fly in all directions. Freedom is the only cry! One standard bears the strange device called *beauty,* another *truth*; and others fly for *recreation, craftsmanship, moral teaching, heritage, skill in language, thought, feeling, music, enjoyment,* or *the poet.* The list is endless and the listing vain. Some standard bearers do not know the meaning of their own devices. For them pursuit is everything. Others grope through a lifetime for some vague sesame, and find at last perhaps a sentiment that mocks them at the grave. Enjoyment in poetry, like beauty in art and peace in politics, is an afterglow. Like humour, it is usually accidental and often inexplicable. It comes unlooked for; it cannot be called. When it is felt, its presence is acknowledged by both the poet and his reader with gratitude and humility. But aim directly at it, either to create it or to claim it, and it vanishes like a dream! To learn a skill, develop a technique, acquire information, find a moral, or while away the time—these aims, although they appear infinitely more practical and immediate, are at best digressions. They lead away from poetry, not to it. Any aim that hopes to reach its goal, to make poetry yield

47

the secret of its power, must be shaped by clearer purposes. Not skill, nor knowledge, nor enjoyment, but poetry itself must be the object of the quest. Not some vain desire to appear either knowing or clever is enough to set the pilgrim on his way. Those who storm the citadel where literary treasures abound require neither a super-sensitive nervous system,[1] nor the mystifying pedantry of the academician, but most of all honesty of purpose, humility of spirit, and courage that dispels pretence. To the reader who possesses these qualities, poetry will not fail to yield at least a little of its power.

Just what treasure a reader may bring back from his quest, there is no telling. Literary values are found in quality, not quantity, in essenccs rather than accounts.

> What would bechance at Lyonnesse
> While I should sojourn there
> No prophet durst declare,
> Nor did the wisest wizard guess
> What would bechance at Lyonnesse
> While I should sojourn there.[2]

There is no instrument to gauge the radiance of poetic fire, but few spirits may come within the range of its brightness or its warmth, and escape its power to transmute.

> When I came back from Lyonnesse
> With magic in my eyes,
> All marked with mute surmise
> My radiance fair and fathomless,
> When I came back from Lyonnesse
> With magic in my eyes![2]

[1] I. A. Richards, *The Principles of Literary Criticism*. Kegan Paul.

[2] *Lyonnesse*. From *Collected Poems of Thomas Hardy*. By permission of Macmillan & Co. Ltd.

Its effect, like its cause, although too deep for understanding, is evident enough to awaken wonder. No one
would venture to predict or guess what might befall the
young knight who journeyed to Lyonnesse, but that he
suffered a change, strange and wonderful, no one who saw
him afterwards would deny. This is identical with the
change that poetry can work in the spirit of its reader, and
any one charged with the responsibility of accompanying
young readers in their quest for poetry should know himself the nature of this change. Any effort spent on its
analysis can hardly be in vain.

So much has been spoken and written about the appreciation of poetry that much of the meaning the term may
once have possessed has been lost in the jargon of pedants.
Anything from a sentimental liking for a poem to an unin-
telligible abstraction about its style has been described as
the appreciation of poetry. Subjective or objective, the aim
or attitude has always been the same—in one way or another to bring poetry into a counting-house, to appraise or
evaluate it, but if poetry is not discovered before it reaches
any tribunal, no matter how sound the laws or how noble
the principles of the judges, its influence will never be
felt. Not in a spirit of criticism, but in one of submission,
is poetry apprehended, and when it is apprehended the
reader suffers a "felt change of consciousness".[1] In proportion to the intensity with which he enters into the
experience of the poem, his own experience is shaped and
controlled. Until the difference between these two potentialities, the spirit of the poem and the spirit of the reader,
is resolved, the reader undergoes an emotional and

---

[1] Owen Barfield, *Poetic Diction*. Faber.

imaginative change with the result that he apprehends within himself a new experience. This is called *poetic experience*. It is initiated by the reading of a poem and is shaped by its contemplation, but it belongs in its essence to the reader. Philologists may teach others the value of words, and psychologists may awaken in others "perceptive sensitivities", but no one can determine fully the character of another's poetic experience. In one way or another a skilful teacher may influence its fulfilment, but the apprehension of poetic experience is a gift of the pupil or the reader.

Before this fact can be accepted, it is necessary to discover first what is meant by experience, and then, if possible, what is meant by poetry. For many people experience is a search for new sensations or impressions. Unless the new adventure provides a "thrill", it is merely another commonplace incident in existence. On this point Aldous Huxley in *Texts and Pretexts* has something significant to say.

> The poet is, etymologically, the maker. Like all makers he requires a stock of raw materials—in his case, experience. Now experience is not a matter of having actually swum the Hellespont, or danced with dervishes, or slept in a doss-house. It is a matter of sensibility and intuition, of seeing and hearing the significant things, of paying attention at the right moments, of understanding and co-ordinating. Experience is not what happens to a man; it is what a man does with what happens to him. It is a gift for dealing with the accidents of existence, not the accidents themselves. By a happy dispensation of nature, the poet generally possesses the gift of experience in conjunction with that of expression. What he says so well is therefore intrinsically of value.

This "gift of experience" enables a man to apprehend intuitively, as it were, the essences of things, and to realize imaginatively the part they play in the drama of his own life. His experience may in every sense of the word be called *real* and the man *alive*. Whether he has beheld a sunset, made a new friendship, fought a forest fire, or learned to fly an aeroplane, he has added to his experience of living and may with Ulysses proclaim

I am a part of all that I have met.

What experience a man apprehends in any act or thing depends on his hereditary impulses, the conditions of his environment, the tenacity of his will, the temper of his soul, and so much more besides that it staggers the mind to contemplate. The physician, the philosopher, and the theologian, all may have something to say about it, but not even the psychologist can guess its character. The apprehension of experience is too subtle for analysis.

It is obvious, too, that not all persons possess the gift of literary experience. Some, for instance, find greater satisfaction in the experience of music, painting, sculpture, or architecture; but let it be remembered that no art gives man a satisfaction comparable with the art of living—no matter how faulty the masterpiece. The art of living is chief of all the arts. It inspires them and may in turn be inspired by them. Life and literature are not two peas in one pod. Through Literature to Life, like Through Life to Literature, is merely another specious slogan. If literature and life must be considered together, it would be wiser to regard life as a tree, and literature as a vine clinging to the tree—a tree that may be made more beautiful because of its vine. Life and literature may enhance each other, but real experience and literary experience are different types of experience. In his essay *Poetry for Poetry's Sake* A. C. Bradley describes them as "different *ways* of feeling". "Poetry and life have different *kinds* of existence. In life we are angry or afraid; in poetry we have sympathetic knowing of what it is to feel anger or fear." This, he believed, is "the difference between *real* and *imaginative* experience", and he perceived what he called an "underground connection" between the two. It is quibbling to argue that in one, reality is informed by imagination; and in the other, imagination is informed by reality: or that in one, man is moved to passion; and in the other, is passionately moved. History has recorded the lives of men who have been rich in real experience, but who have had little or no knowledge of poetry or any of the other arts. Likewise it has recorded the lives of men who were so immersed in at least one of the arts that they floundered like derelicts in the tempests of life. Real experience and literary experience, despite the arguments of I. A. Richards to the contrary, are "different *ways* of feeling"; and history reveals further that some of the wisest men possessed both gifts to a remarkable degree. What these experiences mean to each other may be revealed by an examination of the nature of *poetic* experience.

Many attempts have been made to define poetry, but few to determine its function. The best definitions take their precedence from the personal bias of their creators; the worst are crudely repetitious. All, nevertheless, at some time served some useful purpose. The same may be said of attempts to determine the function of poetry. Conclusions here are no more profound, or generally applicable, than the personal experiences on which they are based. For one generation of readers poetry has no function, unless it be the glorification of itself by the exhalation of an ineffable "beauty"; for another it is the imperishable hope for the salvation of mankind. Among the muddled aberrations of thought that pass for principles today, any attempt to find a use for poetry begs no excuse. In a world in which the importance of material things is grossly exaggerated, a rediscovery of the significance of poetry may do much to restore a balance of interests, if not of power, and to re-establish a sense of proportion in all our thinking. It is futile, however, to confront one exaggeration with another, and between them expect to find some truth either in the conflict of opposites or in the dull stability of exhaustion. At this stage even modest claims for poetry may easily destroy the ends for which they are intended. If its function is to be determined, poetry must be observed in action.

How, then, is poetry created? The poet, endowed with a capacity for intense experience and the ability to give significant expression to his creative impulses, makes it up out of his own speculations and reflections. The nucleus of thought and feeling in which the poem finds its source may be the product of his conscious or unconscious mind. So far his experience is wholly subjective, a flash of light in the brain, a surge of emotion through the body, as the poem yet unborn gropes for its rhythm and its form. Now, with all the technical knowledge and skill of the literary artist, he begins to compose, to make in words a definite objective record of his subjective experience. His aim is always to be exact, to find words that fit precisely his thought and image and mood. This task would be comparatively easy if the thing he is recording would, like a hill, remain fixed before his eye, but it will not. In the restless flow of his creative energy one image suggests another, one idea brings in its wake a whole flurry of new thoughts. Endowed with a critical sense of words, he selects, designs, revises, until he has defined the limits of its changing shape. Of the star by which he set his course he has now only fleeting glimpses in the cloud-strewn sky, but he struggles forward in its general direction with all the tenacity of will at his command. Composition becomes a self-creating process at the end of which stands the poem, and the words of the poem mark the course of the poet's struggle. To the raw materials of his original experience, already transmuted by his imagination, he has added a selection of the materials suggested to him in the spiritual heat of composition. A poem does not spring completed from the poet's brain. He cannot foresee its final form or effect. It is a *composition,* the product of his creative activity, a living record of his experience in the act of creating. As a literary work of art, it has a life and spirit of its own—a spirit born of the poet's spirit. It is ready now to fare forth into the world alone, and the poet retires weary from a labour that refreshes. A poem contains the memory of a mood to which is added the passion of creative effort.

Why the poet creates the poem, is an interesting question. To say that he does it because he cannot help doing it, excludes the will. The poet is essentially a maker, a creator, not a pliant reed. Like the child working with plasticene, he feels the material taking shape in his hands, but he also, if it is to have any meaning for himself, consciously or unconsciously controls the shape it is finally to take. The poet *wills* to create the poem, and he moulds it to the shape of his responsive mind under the pressure of experience. What meaning the finished poem may have for the reader is not the poet's primary concern. At his best he is not primarily a propagandist seeking with the aid of facile rhymes and rhythms to spread some doctrine or preach some moral; he is a poet bent first of all on being true to himself, on preserving from oblivion and death something of his own experience of living. To say that through poetry the poet escapes from life, is a common misconception of the poet's purpose, and often leads to a misunderstanding of the use of poetry. It would be more compatible with truth to say that through poetry he escapes from death, and that consequently in poetry the reader finds a more abundant life.

Again, but with greater insistence than before, comes the question, what is poetry? It must be again denied. It were as easy for a theologian to reduce faith to a formula as for anyone, even the poets themselves, to catch the secret of poetry in a neat definition. It may be "emotion recollected in tranquillity", "the spontaneous overflow of powerful feeling", "the best words in the best order", "the criticism of life", "not the thing said but a way of saying it", "memorable speech", "the record of the best and happiest moments of the happiest and best minds", or "feeling confessing itself to itself in moments of solitude" A poem may possess any one or all of these qualities, but if the reader wishes to find its "poetry" he must seek it in the poem itself. A poem is a single whole made up of many parts—a metrical *composition* of closely integrated elements; and just as life is present in all parts of a living organism, so in the poem poetry, or what may be called poetic experience, exists to some degree in every word.

> Each perfect in its place; and each content
> With that perfection which is being meant.[1]

Take a word out of its context, and at once it is ashen cold and dead; put it back, and it glows as brightly as ever it did, but the reader may now be more aware of the illumination it contributes to the general flame.

> MACBETH: Duncan is in his grave;
> After life's fitful fever he sleeps well;

Taken separately these words have little significance. Even the passage, separated entirely from its context, states simply that Duncan's dead and he's lucky. But replace the passage in its context with Macbeth in full career, and observe the words of the passage taken together, when each word becomes entangled in the meaning, suggestion, feeling, imagery, and rhythm of the whole, and then perceive how language takes on a significance far beyond its dictionary meaning. Words are the poet's only counters in the market of experience. A genuine poem may be found to possess thought, subsidiary meanings, imagery, emotion, sound, rhythm, and form,[2] all of which owe their existence to words, but its poetry is found not in these elements taken separately, but rather in the complex, fully organized whole composed of these elements in fusion. "In a work of art the value of the parts combined into a whole is far greater than the value of the sum of the

[1] J. E. Spingarn.
[2] P. Gurrey, *The Appreciation of Poetry*. Oxford, 1935.

parts."[1] So subtle is the interpenetration of these parts that the reader, like the poet, is lost if he fails to keep his attention riveted to words. In words is crystallized the poet's poetic experience. Coleridge's definition of poetry as "the best words in the best order" emphasizes the importance of words, and T. S. Eliot's definition of poetry as "excellent words in excellent arrangements and excellent metre",[2] although it adds little, proclaims a similar point of view. In the line "After life's fitful fever he sleeps well" Shakespeare attributes as elsewhere to Macbeth a poet's power of thought, feeling, and imagination, but as Macbeth weighs for an instant the relative values of life and death it is impossible to determine completely where thought leaves off and feeling begins, to separate entirely the emotion from the imagery, or to draw a sharp line of distinction between the sound and rhythm and the sense. In genuine poetry all the component elements are so indivisibly interwoven with one another in the words that a single word cannot be added or taken away without impairing the texture or the fabric of the poetry. This is equally true of a verse, a stanza, or a poem as a whole. And what significance a word or a verse may contribute to the whole is to a large extent derived from the whole. "For the Whole is not merely the sum of the parts of which it is made up, nor even the organ in which they perform a function: it is the only true reality."[3]

After life's fitful fever he sleeps well

is a string of simple words, but as spoken by Macbeth

[1] Clive Bell, *Art*. Chatto & Windus, 1914.
[2] T. S. Eliot, *The Sacred Wood*. Methuen.
[3] Lawrence Hyde, *The Prospects of Humanism*.

under the circumstances and especially the time of the action, these words become charged with a power of suggestion that is reserved to poetry alone. For one poet, poetry may be "memorable speech", for another "emotion recollected in tranquillity", for still another "the criticism of life", but for the reader it is a power latent in the words of a poem. By the use of words the poet creates a poem; controlled by the words of the poem, the reader creates poetic experience.

What happens, then, when a reader begins the contemplation of a poem? The answer is precisely nothing, if, for the time being, he has not suspended judgment and set aside his preconceived ideas. Eliot's *The Waste Land* remains a land of waste for those who cannot see beyond the graveyard in Gray's famous *Elegy*. The reader of poetry must approach his task in a spirit of sincere humility, ready to submit to a new control. There is no place here for the effete aristocrat of lettered pretense. And the reading of poetry is a task, and not, as so commonly conceived, a sensuous indulgence. The reading of genuine poetry calls forth the best that is in a man—all his capacities and powers—as someone has said, "with all one's powers at a stretch."

About the best poetry, and not only the best, there floats an atmosphere of infinite suggestion. The poet speaks to us of one thing, but in this one thing there seems to lurk the secret of all. He said what he meant, but his meaning seems to beckon away beyond itself, or rather to expand into something boundless which is only focussed in it; something also which, we feel, would satisfy not only the imagination, but the whole of us.[1]

[1] A. C. Bradley, *Oxford Lectures on Poetry*, 1909. By permission of Macmillan & Co. Ltd.

In these words A. C. Bradley directs our attention in poetry to what is unuttered but expressed. I. A. Richards, on the other hand, in his *Principles of Literary Criticism,* would have us believe that the use of poetry is to stimulate and develop the health of our nervous systems, to make our sense of awareness more acute. He is apparently not *aware* of the human misery, let alone the human monstrosities, that would follow in the wake of his advice, were it possible to accept and practise his theories. Like so many psychologists, he cannot see the forest for the experimental trees, and appears to be unable to recognize the mind as a co-ordinating agent of experience, or as Coleridge described it, as "a living and growing, self-creating process." The human senses are alert enough; what they await is a spirit, to direct them! Were they not alert, what could the psychologist, who has long since lost sight of *psyche,* do about it—separate the quick from the dead? Precisely! Unless my sense of hearing deceives me, I hear the ticking echo of a "scientific" time-piece measuring response. "Quickness", someone has said, "is among the least of the mind's properties, and belongs to her in almost her lowest state: nay, it doth not abandon her when she is driven from her home, when she is wandering and insane. The mad often retain it; the liar has it, the cheat has it; we find it on the race-course and at the card-table: education does not give it, and reflection takes it away." Does the purification of the human spirit depend upon the perfecting of the processes of the nervous system? Is a quick muscle always a sign of a quickened spirit? The ability of the "intellectual" to pick up half-truths and to make what are called "snap-judgments" is not one of the qualifications of the reader of poetry, but a readiness to submit to the control of words in poetry is undeniably a prerequisite. The reader must surrender his forces to the will of the poet and marshal his own experiences to march in line with the disciplined words of the poem. Unless he submits to these limitations, the reader's creative energies are squandered in fugitive speculations and his spirit cannot identify itself with the spirit the poet left behind in the poem.

"Art relies for its full effect upon what the spectator brings with him."[1] In the process of studying or contemplating the words of the poem in their poetic order, the reader is gradually and continuously apprehending and assimilating the poetic experience of the poem, both by adjusting his own experience to that which is latent in the words of the poem, and by comprehending entirely new experiences in the process of co-ordination. In this process the reader's interests and instincts, his speculations and reflections, are sublimated, organized, intensified, and sometimes even dramatized in his imagination. True, his senses may be quickened and sharpened by this activity, but what really matters is the extent to which he experiences a "qualitative inner change". It is absurd to say that the reader recreates the original experience of the poet. The poet himself could hardly do that once his original perspective and pattern of thought and feeling had faded away. On this point any poet's objective revision of his own work is an interesting commentary and proof enough. Even a prolonged interruption in the process of creating may throw a poet off his stride. But what the reader does is to create an experience that

[1] Greville Cooke, *Art and Reality*.   J. Williams.

approximates the experience left by the poet in the poem. According to what the reader "brings with him", he apprehends and assimilates something of what the poet originally or creatively experienced, and the reader, at the end of this creative process, is in possession of a new poetic experience.

"All creative activity is unforeseeable."[1] Just what shape the reader's poetic experience will take is unpredictable. In character, it varies with his age and the amount of real experience he has assimilated. In depth or intensity, it varies with the natural cast of his mind and the amount of practice he has had in apprehending imaginative experience. Even the nature of the English language may have something to do with it. This Attic Greek of modern times admits of varying response for different readers. What does not vary, however, is the poem. Its words stand guard forever at their allotted stations. They may bleach and tarnish in the weather of time, but the spirit that informs their order is imperishable. A page of Shakespeare or of Milton is proof enough of this, but

> What would bechance at Lyonnesse
> While I should sojourn there
> No prophet durst declare,
> Nor did the wisest wizard guess
> What would bechance at Lyonnesse
> While I should sojourn there.

If, then, it may be assumed that poetic experience has some value and that its apprehension and assimilation provide an activity that is worth cultivating, what is the

[1] G. Rostrevor Hamilton, *Poetry and Contemplation*. Cambridge, 1937.

function of the teacher who is working with a class of inexperienced readers? If he fancies himself as an exhibitor of literary works, he will, with due academic condescension, conduct his charges on a tour of the masterpiece. Here and there he may snipe at a word or a rhythm with an arrow of cleverness from some critic's quiver. If he is a literary technician, he will aim to mystify his pupils by conjuring with what he calls literary tricks and devices. Hyperbole and metonymy are representative of his jargon. If he believes in an approach through psychology, he will aim to increase the "awareness" of his pupils, to "sensitize" their nervous systems, to awaken their "perceptive sensibilities". Should he imagine himself to be a philosopher of the subject, he will regard the work of art as an historical document and attempt to explain its position in some literary cycle. If he pretends to be a connoisseur of the arts, he will expound the aesthetics of poetry. Like the moralist with his very private set of ethical principles, he will commend or condemn according to his likes or dislikes. If he belongs to the intelligentsia he will ferret out the thought-content of the poem and try to clarify its meaning by pursuing its logical sequence to its final statement. He will intellectualize the poem and propound critical judgments on its social implications. For him the poem is a social document; and if possible he will "school" the poem to fit his preconceived theories of its purpose. His aim will be to put the muse in chains and to stand complacently in the poet's light.

The first thing for the teacher of poetry to remember is to forget himself. He is a guide to those in search of literary experience, but he must also play the part of codiscoverer. He is a leader who knows best how to follow, how to keep out of his own light by keeping out of the light of his companions. He merely nods direction, and stimulates the pace. Having been this way before, he knows best how to take advantage of every beauty of surprise, how to read each image, sound, and rhythm as it comes, and how to plan for the effect to which each thought and feeling must lead on. By his own zeal he inspires confidence in his fellows. By his own insight he awakens their intuitive powers. By his own faith he inspires their belief. They submit to the discipline of the search and surrender their impulses to the poet's order. As their full mental responses are controlled and shaped by the poem, their poetic experiences are in the process of being formed. The teacher of poetry must therefore understand the process by which a poem becomes a work of creative art. He must also understand something of the process by which the pupils assimilate imaginative experience and translate it into conscious action. But he fails completely if he does not understand the nature of his own function in the process by which his pupils apprehend poetic experience. Rightly conceived and exercised, his function may become an art, an art that in its aim and effect conceals the artist and his skill.

Like an artist, the teacher of poetry begins with his own subjective experience of the object he contemplates, namely the poem. Like an art, his achievement produces its ultimate effect in the very personal subjective experience of the observer, namely the pupil. What, then, are some of the principal manifestations of his skill as he explores the poem with his class? From the beginning to the end of the search he aims to keep the pupil's mind preoccupied with the poem; to give the poem a sympathetic, interpretative reading; to preserve the organic unity of the poem as a work of creative art; to regard the poem as objectively as he can, despite the fact that at almost every turn his own personality is likely to get entangled with what he teaches; to follow carefully the main sequence of the poem, analyzing, integrating, and synthesizing as the search proceeds; to lead the pupils away from the by-paths of fugitive speculation and into the highway of self-realization through faithful interpretation; to invite the contemplation of the significance of this sound, the suggestion of that rhythm, the steadying influence of this image on the thought, the stimulating effect of that figurative language on the mood, the limits or boundaries set by this metre, the uniqueness of this passage of memorable speech, and the completeness and finality of this form; to gather up the materials of the poem in an orderly way, and to hold them in solution, as it were, until their precipitation begins to form in a cumulative effect.

Realizing that the better part of this effect is subjective and personal for each member of his class, the teacher will not try to control its shape, but only to assure its purity by holding the poem (to change the metaphor) in sunlit suspension until it can be clearly seen by all. Realizing that "the experience of a poem matures at the end of a vital process, and is what it is because of that process,"[1] he will aim to secure the best possible conditions for the development of that process. He will try to win the response of the pupil's inward consciousness to the inward, spiritualized faith or love or hope or courage (whatever it

[1] *Poetry and Contemplation.*

may be) that is the controlling and informing life of the poem. He will bring the pupil as far as possible into the mood that moulds the poem, as near as possible to the height of its tension, as deeply as possible into a consciousness of the eternal fitness of its language, so that the spirit of the pupil may, by a sudden leap of sympathy and intuition from within, come into contact with the spirit of the poem.

Once we touch a transcendental, we touch being itself, a likeness of God, an absolute, all that ennobles and makes the joy of life: we enter the realm of the spirit. It is remarkable that the only real means of communication between human creatures is through being or some one of the properties of being. This is their only means of escape from the individuality in which they are enclosed by matter. If they remain on the plane of their sensible needs and their sentimental selves, they tell their stories to one another in vain; they cannot understand each other. They watch each other and cannot see, each infinitely alone, however closely work or the pleasure of love may bind them together. But once touch the good and Love, like the Saints, or the true, like an Aristotle, or the beautiful, like a Dante, a Bach or a Giotto, then contact is established and souls communicate. Men are only really united by the spirit . . .[1]

Until this leap is taken the energizing force of poetry lies dormant in the frozen symbols on the printed page, and "poetry as communication" is only a myth sung at a wishing well too full for sound. Once this contact is made, the mind may direct the intellect and the emotions in the building of a bridge across the divide, and the poet at last may be in direct communication with the pupil. In the process by which the pupil builds this bridge, the function of the teacher is extremely important. He asks the pupil to test the validity and vitality of the dynamic details that

[1] Jacques Maritain, *Art and Scholasticism.*

contribute collectively to the mood and spirit of the poem as a living organism, to bear witness to their infallible aptness, to walk forth "on his own shadow"[1] until his shadow is lost in the substance of the poem. Safety for the average person lies in using "the creations of art as means for confirming and strengthening his own personal apprehensions. Books, poems, and pictures should serve for him as agencies for bringing into the full light of consciousness that which the mind already in some sense possesses, but has not yet properly mastered. They should promote the crystallization into form of impressions and ideas which have their source in deep and personal experience. They should aid in solving a problem, in attaining to a profound synthesis, in achieving a fuller degree of self-realization. We should look outside ourselves in order to complete a process which has been initiated within."[2] But to do this we must cross the divide, and not content ourselves merely with beholding the hills from afar.

In another way and for another purpose Gerard Manley Hopkins once expressed much the same idea:

It is a happy thing that there is no royal road to poetry. The world should know by this time that one cannot reach Parnassus except by flying thither. Yet from time to time more men go up and either perish in its gullies fluttering excelsior flags or else come down again with full folios and blank countenances. Yet the old fallacy keeps its ground. Every age has its false alarms.

The aim of the teacher, who has the power to inspire others with zeal for the discovery of poetic experience, is

[1] "No man can walk abroad save on his own shadow."—SIR WALTER RALEIGH.

[2] *The Prospects of Humanism.*

not to fill with facts and lifeless abstractions the notebooks
of his pupils, but to quicken their spirits. It is not to stuff
their mouths with sawdust, but to give them good fruit
from the vine that clings to the tree of life. It is not to
darken their countenances with the futility of arid intellectualism or of arrant emotionalism, but to evoke from
their spirits a "radiance fair and fathomless". His aim is
not that of the psychologist who invites introspection and
turns the pupil inward to consume himself in swampy
places, but rather it is that of the poet who invites the pupil
to go forth by a prescribed course to inhabit the spacious
hills. The object of the teacher is to secure a balance
between the cold, calculating, sceptical intellect and the
warm, sympathetic, eager intuition; to sublimate the
instincts to the order of the mind; to achieve in some
degree the integration of consciousness and being. If
the pupil will put forth in cheerful faith with all his
powers—body, mind, and soul—at the stretch, he may
glimpse the far horizons of the spirit to which the intellect
by itself is blind. He may acquire little knowledge, but he
will breathe "the breath and finer spirit of all knowledge".
His powers will be integrated and his mind re-organized
by the work of art he contemplates. He will achieve a
freedom, the true liberty, that puts to shame the license
of the false humanist. The appreciation of poetry is an
experience of forthgoing into a realm more significant
and satisfying than that of one's own insular and self-
regarding individuality.

To secure the highest possible accuracy and efficiency
in the ripening process in which the pupil exercises his
powers of co-ordination and adjusts himself to the poem,

the teacher must preserve a firm sense of perspective, proportion, orderliness, and restraint. The depth and intensity of the pupil's subjective experience will depend to a great degree on the teacher's controlled objective analysis and synthesis of the experience within the poem. For all his goodwill and sympathy the teacher must make sure that the poem does not pass across the pupil's mind, but into it, that it becomes an experience lived through, something possessing and possessed. In the performance of this ritual the teacher will be guided by his own honest and sincere belief, insight, and inspiration, and not alone by someone else's opinions. The influence of literary criticism on the cultivation of appreciation is sometimes subversive. But the teacher must guarantee to his pupils the right to rise above him within the prescribed limits of the poem, if, of course, they can find a place to perch at the end of their flight. It may be well to recall the advice of a wise Persian poet of ancient days on the training of children:

You may give them your love but not your thoughts,
For they have their own thoughts.
You may house their bodies but not their souls,
For their souls dwell in the House of Tomorrow.
You may strive to be like them, but seek not to make them like you;
For life goes not backward nor tarries with yesterday.

But fugitive speculation should not be permitted. Furthermore the pupil's mind should not be allowed to become cluttered or preoccupied with abstractions "and correspondingly unreceptive to the significant and unanalyzable immediacies".[1]

[2] *The Prospects of Humanism.*

For, after all, a poem is a poem not least by virtue of its power to ward off these vagaries of the intellect. It is to some degree an incantation, a word of immediate power, compelling the wandering mind to response of a certain order; and only so far as the receiving mind restrains its speculations within the limits of this order is it speculating about the poem at all.[1]

Without restraint there can be no profundity; without control, no decent spontaneity; without order, no organic and creative living; and without submission, no freedom in forthgoing. There can be no half-way measures with poetry; it demands our all. The poet, however, must never be mistaken for God, or the practice and study of his art (or of any other art for that matter) be allowed to become a substitute for religion. The absolute of all values is God. The poet may inspire man to look beyond himself for salvation, may awaken his soul and quicken his spirit, may, indeed, force man to come to grips with himself, but he cannot save man's soul. The priest, or the pastor, thinks downward from the transcendental God; the poet thinks upward through the immanence of God. Divine grace comes from above and not from beneath. It originates with God in heaven; art originates with men on earth. Art may be the true earthly reality—the nearest thing to perfection of which the human mind is capable. At its highest peak it may receive and reflect divine effulgence. But it can never be the primal cause of that glory that comes only from afar.

Inspiration is not a mythological accessory only. There is a real inspiration, proceeding not from the Muses, but from the living God, a special impulse of the natural order, whereby the first Mind gives the artist, when it pleases, a creative impulse transcending the limits of reason and employing as it elevates every rational energy

---

[1] *The Prospects of Humanism.*

of art. Man of his free will can obey or destroy such an impetus. This inspiration which descends from God, the author of nature, is as it were a symbol of supernatural inspiration. For an art to arise which shall be Christian not only in hope but in fact, truly freed by grace, both forms of inspiration will have to be united at its most secret source.[1]

The great poets, when their souls receive through the agency of their valiant spirits a vision and a voice divine, become the imitators of God and the witnesses of his creation.

Of her "own best poets" Elizabeth Barrett Browning wrote in *Aurora Leigh*:

> I write so
> Of the only truth-tellers now left to God,
> The only speakers of essential truth,
> Opposed to relative, comparative,
> And temporal truths; the only holders by
> His sun-skirts, through conventional grey glooms;
> The only teachers who instruct mankind
> From just a shadow on a charnel-wall
> To find man's veritable stature out
> Erect, sublime,—the measure of a man,
> And that's the measure of an angel, says
> The apostle. Aye, and while your common men
> Lay telegraphs, gauge railroads, reign, reap, dine,
> And dust the flaunty carpets of the world
> For kings to walk on, or our president,
> The poet suddenly will catch them up
> With his voice like a thunder,—'This is soul,
> This is life, this word is being said in heaven,
> Here's God down on us! what are you about?'
> How all those workers start amid their work,
> Look round, look up, and feel, a moment's space,
> That carpet-dusting, though a pretty trade,
> Is not the imperative labour after all.

[1] *Art and Scholasticism.*

Nothing could be more harmful, however, than to spread abroad an exaggerated idea of poetry as a spiritualizing agent, a plan for a philosophy of life, or a vehicle for choral speaking. Its appeal is not made through any one of its parts taken separately, but through the whole. The reader does not, for instance, begin with the images, or end with the sounds. He begins with the title or the first line, and he ends with the solution of the whole problem with which the poet has confronted him. His interest may be awakened by the nature of the subject, but it is sustained by the exercise of his own mental and spiritual faculties in the contemplation of the poem. His interest is rewarded partly by his own achievement in the *reading* of words. The value and the significance of words are the bases of all profitable study in both appreciation and composition.

When we begin to discover that the poet's words work on our minds in this way, when we begin to be conscious that his words give us impressions of the qualities of things, and at the same time that they express those impressions for us, and that this expression has for us a certain degree of completeness, accuracy, and insight, then we have begun to be aware of words aesthetically; we have begun to be aware of words as an artistic medium, as material which can reveal a beauty of form to us.[1]

The intensive reading of poetry for the sake of apprehending literary experience is, like education, a process not only of unfolding, leading out, and enlightening, but also of controlling, training, and moulding. Any lasting benefit that may accrue to society from either poetry

[1] *The Appreciation of Poetry.*

or education can come only through the personal action
and reaction of the individual.

In the study of English literature the pendulum has
swung from one extreme to another, from the old analysis
for the sake of analysis to the new freedom of choice for
enjoyment. One of the purposes of this book is to point
to a way by which we may again find our equilibrium by
finding the centre. It recommends an emphasis on the
core rather than the periphery of man's true nature, and
in spite of the present-day convention of exploratory
courses in English, it invites the substitution of "vertical
penetration" for "indefinite horizontal expansion".

In the practice of the methods of study illustrated in
this book, the pupil's tastes and powers of discrimination
are quickly improved. If a light fanciful lyric lacks the
substance of fancy, its hollowness is soon discovered. If
the poet's insight falls short of its mark, his fault is soon
apparent. If the form and the substance of poetry meet
in the creation of imaginative experience, the pupil
acknowledges the magic of inspired art. "In their flashes
of insight taste and genius are one."[1]

The identity of genius and taste is the final achievement of
modern thought on the subject of art, and it means that fundamentally, in their most significant moments, the creative and the
critical instincts are one and the same.[2]

From what has already been said, it is apparent that the
responsibilities of the teacher of English are not lighter
than those of the teachers of other subjects. His only
hope, however, lies in his being true to the best that is in

[1] J. E. Spingarn, *Creative Criticism*.
[2] Ibid.

him—in being fastidious in his aim and forthright in his function. But before we submit him to examination, we shall observe the process in which he plays his part— believing, as we do, that "anyone who has ever been visited by the Muse is thenceforth haunted."[1]

[1] T. S. Eliot, *The Use of Poetry and The Use of Criticism.* Faber.

Chapter Three

TO AUTUMN

THIS lesson, like those that follow it, is the result of work done some years ago with a class of average senior secondary school pupils trained in this method. An effort has been made to preserve the main development of each lesson—the content and the sequence rather than the form of the pupils' answers. Here and there, to save space and pointedness, the ideas expressed in several short answers have been combined into a composite answer worded by the teacher. This method can be adapted easily to the needs of pupils of other grades, provided the material of the lesson is suitable for the grade.

The poems selected here for study are intended to be representative of those commonly found in school anthologies. Some of them, the reader will admit, are excellent works of art. The teacher's subjective preferences, however, enter very little into this problem.

It will be obvious to all that these lessons are carefully planned in a way that is easily adaptable to the changing needs of a class. Very little is left to chance. The questions are not always easy to make, but the answers are often easy to find in the poem and in the pupils' reactions to it. One purpose of the questions is to cultivate the pupils' minds, to keep the pupils on their mental toes and imaginatively reaching. Another purpose is to provide food for contemplation more nourishing than the product of wool-gathering. Still another purpose is to allow time for their experiences to grow and their spiritual muscles to develop. A delayed response of any kind is hardly possible where there has been no initial contact.

The lesson material is consequently not a catechism, but an exposition of a method that is based on the theory that to know anything well one must ask the right questions about it—not just any questions or a prescribed set of questions, but the right questions. Eventually the pupils will learn by training how to ask their own questions.

T. In the late afternoon of Sunday, September 19, 1819, John Keats, a young English poet, went for a walk in the pastures and stubble-fields near Winchester in Hampshire. The autumn weather and its effect on the country-side made a deep impression on him, and because he was a poet, thoughts, feelings, and images began, we may suppose, to take shape in his mind in the form of rhythmic groups of words. The impression that he had received was so intense that the single mood that dominated him at that time remained with him, and four days later he completed the poem we are about to read—*To Autumn.*

(The teacher reads the poem aloud slowly and rhythmically, giving full value to the vowels and consonants.)

> Season of mists and mellow fruitfulness,
>   Close bosom-friend of the maturing sun;
> Conspiring with him how to load and bless
>   With fruit the vines that round the thatch-eaves run;
> To bend with apples the moss'd cottage-trees,
>   And fill all fruit with ripeness to the core;
>   To swell the gourd, and plump the hazel shells
>   With a sweet kernel; to set budding more,
> And still more, later flowers for the bees,
> Until they think warm days will never cease,
>   For Summer has o'er-brimm'd their clammy cells.

Who hath not seen thee oft amid thy store?
    Sometimes whoever seeks abroad may find
Thee sitting careless on a granary floor,
    Thy hair soft-lifted by the winnowing wind,
Or on a half-reap'd furrow sound asleep,
    Drowsed with the fume of poppies, while thy hook
        Spares the next swath and all its twinèd flowers;
And sometimes like a gleaner thou dost keep
    Steady thy laden head across a brook;
    Or by a cider-press, with patient look,
        Thou watchest the last oozings hours by hours.

Where are the songs of Spring?   Ay, where are they?
    Think not of them, thou hast thy music too,—
While barrèd clouds bloom the soft-dying day,
    And touch the stubble-plains with rosy hue;
Then in a wailful choir the small gnats mourn
    Among the river sallows, borne aloft
        Or sinking as the light wind lives or dies;
And full-grown lambs loud bleat from hilly bourn;
Hedge-crickets sing; and now with treble soft
The redbreast whistles from a garden-croft;
    And gathering swallows twitter in the skies.

T. Nowhere in the poem does Keats tell us directly how he felt, and yet if we read carefully, letting Keats fill our minds with his poem, we can discover how he felt. Read the poem yourselves.   Try to see and hear and feel all that Keats experienced.   You may discover the poet's mood.

(Pupils read silently.)

T. What have you discovered?

P. Keats's mind was full of autumn.   All the things he mentions must have pleased him very much.

P. He must have liked autumn better than any other season.

P. The whole poem deals with autumn—with the things seen and heard at that time of year. Autumn seems to have cast a spell on him; he could think of nothing else.

T. The poem is a unit of thought and feeling. What single word may be used to describe our feelings when by some very great pleasure we are "carried away", or absorbed, or exalted?

P. Joy.

P. Delight.

P. Rapture.

T. These are good words. We may add another, a word derived from Greek, the word *ecstasy,* which means an exalted state of feeling, a feeling that stands out above all others. Possessed of the pleasure he derived from the contemplation of autumn, Keats felt exalted, even transported. But we must define his pleasure more precisely, if we are to discover the mood in which this poem was created. Read again the first two lines of the poem. See if you can discover whether Keats experienced an excited or a sober delight.

> Season of mists and mellow fruitfulness,
>   Close bosom-friend of the maturing sun;

P. He felt a quiet and deep delight.

T. How do you know?

P. There is nothing here that is suddenly exciting. The lines move quietly. The sounds are "mellow".

T. The poet appears to be describing autumn. He has really imparted to us some of the sober delight he felt as he walked across the warm stubble fields. Herein lies one of the chief distinctions between the mind of a great poet and that of an ordinary person, like any one of us. The poet with his mind saturated with his subject stands fearlessly aloof, detached, in the very midst of his ecstasy. No matter how strong or swift his feelings, they are controlling, not consuming. He analyses, selects, and names the sources and the characteristics of his delight. In his imagination he arranges them. As his experience is being thus condensed and its elements are being combined or synthesized, his mood dictates the rhythm or tune, and presently his mood, with all its attendant ideas and images, is crystallized in words. In this poem the poet has declared himself in the opening lines. By what word in the first line does he give us a typical image or glimpse of autumn?

P. Mists are characteristic of autumn.

T. By what words has he crystallized some of the more abstract qualities of the season?

P. Mellow fruitfulness.

T. You said earlier that the lines moved quietly. If we scan the line:

> Season of mists and mellow fruitfulness,

we find that it is not the iambic metre, even with the substitution of a spondaic foot, that makes the rhythm move slowly, but rather it is the presence of long vowels in both accented and unaccented syllables. Keats has enriched both sense and sound by clothing the rhythm in the right succession of consonants and vowels. (The line is read again precisely.) In these observations we have discovered that in image, idea, suggestion and sound Keats has imparted his own sober and secure delight. In

the first line Keats addresses an abstract idea, Season.
How does he make this idea concrete in the second line?

P. He uses the word "friend".

T. How does he define the intimate personal quality of
this friendship?

P. He says the Autumn is a "close bosom-friend".

T. We see here a characteristic of Keats's diction. He
was fond of compound words. What does he gain by the
use of this compound?

P. It fits his meaning more exactly or precisely.

P. It gives a finer shade of meaning.

T. Of what is Autumn a friend?

P. It is a friend of the "maturing sun".

T. Does the word "maturing" describe the sun or a
quality inherent in the sun?

P. It describes the sun.

P. It describes the power of the sun to make things
grow.

P. It describes both; it is the autumn sun that makes
things ripen.

T. Why is *maturing* a better word here than *naturing,*
which appeared in the original version?

P. It places the emphasis on the effect of the sun.

T. This idea still further reinforces the impression con-
veyed in "mellow fruitfulness". If Autumn is a friend of
the sun we must imagine Autumn to be some kind of
god or goddess, but this is not at all clear. All that we can
discover is that the season and the sun are friends.

> Conspiring with him how to load and bless
>> With fruit the vines that round the thatch-eaves run;

Which word here explains further the nature of their friendship?

P. The word "conspiring" suggests that they are secretly scheming together.

T. What are they *conspiring* to do?

P.

—to load and bless
With fruit the vines that round the thatch-eaves run;

T. With what distinction in meaning does Keats use "load" and "bless" in this context?

P. To *load* means to put a great many bunches of grapes on the vines; to *bless* the vines with fruit must mean to put on them an abundance of good fruit.

T. In the original version Keats wrote "The vines with fruit". Why is the revised version better?

P. The arrangement of images is more logical, and the emphasis falls where it should—on "fruit".

T. Keats infers that the harvest will be both great in quantity and high in quality. What is the next thing the sun and the season are conspiring to do?

P.

To bend with apples the moss'd cottage-trees.

T. Observing the position of "bend" in this line, sound the whole line to yourself. What image does it suggest to you?

P. It suggests bent boughs heavily laden with fruit.

T. What else are they planning to do?

P.

And fill all fruit with ripeness to the core;

T. In which does Keats appear to be chiefly interested— the quantity or the quality of the harvest—in this line?

P. He is thinking of the quality of the fruit that is filled with ripeness to the core.

T. Why is *ripeness* a better word than *sweetness* which appeared in the original version?

P. Ripeness suggests more of the quality of the fruit than *sweetness* does.

P. It also is in keeping with the quality of the season and the poet's mood.

T. Much of the richness and suggestiveness of this line is due to the presence in the same phrase of an abstract term *ripeness* and a concrete one *core*. Similar combinations may be found in the poetry of Spenser, Shakespeare, and Milton, in which Keats's mind was steeped. Keats is not content merely to name things; he must name abstract qualities. In this stanza where is the first indication of this intensity of penetration?

P. "Mellow fruitfulness".

T. In the next passage

> To swell the gourd, and plump the hazel shells
> With a sweet kernel

the imagery may be obscured by the presence of an unfamiliar word: a *gourd* is any member of the family of quick-growing plants to which belong the melon and the pumpkin. The fruit of the gourd matures rapidly in the autumn. Why are the verbs "swell" and "plump" particularly apt in this context?

P. In sound and meaning they suggest that the gourd and the shells are filling rapidly with fruit and sweet meat to the point of bursting.

T. When revising, Keats changed *"white* kernel" to *"sweet* kernel". Why is *sweet* the better word?

P. It appeals to the sense of tasting.

T. The images in the remainder of the stanza I shall leave for you to discover from the exact words by which they are expressed.

(At this point the pupils readily select the elements that express or suggest the idea of quantity or of quality. They often show a fine appreciation of such terms as "set budding", "still more", "later flowers", "never cease", and "o'er-brimmed". Even the rhyme *bees* and *cease* draws comment. The only word that offers difficulty is "clammy", and this is soon cleared away when someone discovers the aptness of the word as descriptive of the feeling of the wax of the honeycomb.)

Read the whole stanza silently, giving attention to the verbs and adjectives. (*Allow time for study.*) What meaning is common to the verbs?

P. They all suggest an overflowing abundance.

T. What meaning do the adjectives supply?

P. They describe the sweet, warm, mellow ripeness of the fruits.

T. Read the stanza aloud, emphasizing slightly the words that suggest to you the quantity and quality of the harvest. Try in your reading to give expression to the meaning and the music of the stanza, and to the poet's feeling.

P.

> Season of *mists* and *mellow fruitfulness,*
>> *Close bosom-friend* of the *maturing* sun;
>> *Conspiring* with him *how* to *load* and *bless*
>> With fruit the vines that round the thatch-eaves run;

To *bend* with apples the *moss'd* cottage-trees,
And *fill all fruit with ripeness to the core*;
To *swell* the gourd, and *plump* the hazel shells
With a *sweet* kernel; to *set budding* more,
And *still more, later flowers* for the bees,
Until they think *warm* days will *never cease*,
For Summer has *o'er brimm'd* their *clammy cells*.

T. As you read, I noticed that you paused slightly at the end of each of the first six lines, but that in your reading of the remainder of the stanza you paid less attention to the line-lengths. In pitch, at least, you carried the thought forward from one line into the following one,

—and plump the hazel shells
With a sweet kernel; to set budding more,
And still more, later flowers for the bees,

as if you could not stop until you had reached the last word "cells". What made you do that?

P. The thought is all one piece—one long sentence in the form of an address or apostrophe to the Season. The ideas are piled one on top of the other.

T. You will find the *reason* not only in the thought, but also in the feeling. The poet shows a greater eagerness in these lines. Why does his emotion or feeling appear to move at a higher pitch?

P. It may be that he feels that he cannot say all that he wishes to say in a small space.

T. It appears that the poet is straining against the restriction of the line-length. In both the thought-pattern and the rhythmic movement his expression runs over from one line to another. Evidence of this emotional condition can also be found in the stanza form. In both the *Ode to a Nightingale* and the *Ode on a Grecian Urn,* Keats used a stanza form composed of a quatrain and a sestet: *a b a b, c d e, c d e* (with line 8 shortened), in the former, and *a b a b, c d e, d c e,* in the latter. What form has he used in this great Ode?

P. a b a b, c d e, d c c e.

T. In haste we might assume that this extra line, the tenth, was an addition forced upon the poet by the nature of his subject. For an explanation of this condition we must look beyond the subject to the feelings of the poet. With what feelings did he contemplate the overflowing abundance of the autumn season?

P. He felt intense delight.

T. Considering the stanza as a whole, in how many ways has he shown his delight? Begin with the subject-matter.

P. In one long apostrophe he has given us a number of little pictures or images in rapid succession.

P. The sounds of many of the words, like "mellow", "maturing", "mossed", and "o'er-brimm'd", are appropriate to the subject and reveal Keats's enjoyment of the things he saw and felt.

P. All the verbs state that the harvest will be plentiful.

T. How has the poet's indulgence in his subject affected his feelings?

P. He becomes more excited as he proceeds. His thought begins to run over from one line into the next. He introduces an extra line as if he were working up to a climax.

T. By extending the stanza-form he gained not only an extra line, but also a rhyming couplet, *c c.* Why is this rhyme appropriate near the end of the stanza or at the climax of the feeling?

P. It makes the ending smooth—more musical. It intensifies the higher pitch of the poet's feelings at the end of the stanza.

P. By introducing the extra rhyme, *c c,* he postpones for a whole line the regular rhyme *e,* and this increases the impression of abundance.

T. With penetrating insight Keats has discovered the character and quality of the autumn season, and by his choice and arrangement of words, as well as by his varied rhymes and rhythms, and stanza-form, he has caught in words the quiet and intense delight he felt as he contemplated autumn's rich and ripe abundance.

T.

Who hath not seen thee oft amid thy store?
    Sometimes whoever seeks abroad may find
Thee sitting careless on a granary floor,
    Thy hair soft-lifted by the winnowing wind;
Or on a half-reaped furrow sound asleep,
    Drowsed with the fume of poppies, while thy hook
        Spares the next swath and all its twinèd flowers:
And sometimes like a gleaner thou dost keep
    Steady thy laden head across a brook;
Or by a cider-press, with patient look,
    Thou watchest the last oozings hours by hours.

By what words in the first line is the thought-sequence between the stanzas maintained?

P. "Thee" refers to Autumn and "thy store" to the abundance of the season's harvest.

T. In the next line the poet infers that signs of Autumn may be seen by anyone who cares to look about him. The spirit of Autumn is everywhere. Where in particular does the poet imagine that he sees the incarnation of this spirit?

P. He sees the figure of Autumn sitting on a granary floor.

T. By what word does he describe the typical attitude or mood of Autumn?

P. "Careless".

T. To *winnow* means to blow the chaff or husks from the kernels of grain. Sound this line to yourselves. How is the image of Autumn still further clarified by the rhythm of this line?

P. Autumn appears to be sitting in the grain from which the chaff is being blown. The rhythm of the line imitates the waving of his long hair in the wind:

> Thy hair soft-lifted by the winnowing wind.

T. Where next is the figure of Autumn seen?

P. Autumn has fallen asleep in the harvest field.

T. Just when did Autumn fall asleep?

P. Autumn was overcome by the fume of poppies and fell asleep in the midst of the work, just as the scythe or cradle was about to enter another swath.

T. What words by sound or meaning sustain the idea that Autumn is overcome by the intoxicating fumes of a rank growth?

P. "Sound asleep"; "drowsed"; "fume of poppies"; "spares"; "swath"; and "twinèd".

P. Even the movement of the lines is enough to make me feel the drowsy atmosphere.

T. Why is the revised version better than the original:

> Or sound asleep in a half reaped field
> Dos'd with red poppies.

P. In both sound and rhythm the line is improved. The effect of the sleep-inducing "fume" of the poppies is intensified by "drowsed".

T. All these words are in sound and emotional suggestion in keeping with the mood of Autumn; but Keats is not yet satisfied. Where next does he see Autumn?

P. He imagines he sees Autumn in the form of a harvester, with head laden with gleanings, walking carefully across a brook.

T. In how many ways is the word "steady" appropriate to the context here?

P. The harvester is probably stepping from stone to stone across the partially dry brook.

P. "Steady" also suggests that Autumn personified is heavily laden and moves slowly under the burden.

P. Emphasis is placed on this word by placing it at the beginning of the line.

T. Like "careless", "drowsed", and "twinèd" in their contexts, the word "steady" in this context not only describes a condition, but sustains the mood of Autumn and reveals the sensitiveness of the poet to the images he is presenting. Without these poetic words and drowsy rhythms, these statements would be little better than prose. Keats sees Autumn once again. Read the lines which close the stanza and tell me what image-shaping words or sounds you find.

P. "Patient" expresses an attitude consistent with the mood of Autumn; the sounds in the last line:

> Thou watchest the last oozings hours by hours.

are in keeping with the languor sometimes associated with the season. Here the repetition of the sound *st* delays the delivery and the repetition of the sound *ours* prolongs it.

T. What is contributed in this stanza by the extra line?

P. It provides the poet with additional space in which to draw out the characteristics of the season. The form of the stanza must again give way to the substance.

T. How is this idea still further reinforced by the changed order of the rhyme scheme in this stanza?

P. The poet is more concerned with his images and their postures than he is with the maintenance of a regularity of rhymes.

T. Keats once said of Byron: "He describes what he sees—I describe what I imagine. Mine is the hardest task." What evidence can you find of his skill in this stanza?

P. He imagines that he sees the figure of Autumn in four of his characteristic attitudes. He is more interested in unveiling the spirit of the season than in describing an autumnal scene.

T. How has he bound these "attitudes" together, and given unity to the stanza?

P. Through the whole stanza runs the feeling of drowsy satisfaction.

T. Whence came this feeling?

P. It came from the poet. It is the same feeling of intense delight with which he viewed the abundance of Autumn in the first stanza.

T.

> Where are the songs of Spring? Ay, where are they?
>   Think not of them, thou hast thy music too,—
> While barrèd clouds bloom the soft-dying day,
>   And touch the stubble-plains with rosy hue;
> Then in a wailful choir the small gnats mourn
>   Among the river sallows, borne aloft
>   Or sinking as the light wind lives or dies;
> And full-grown lambs loud bleat from hilly bourn;
>   Hedge-crickets sing; and now with treble soft
> The redbreast whistles from a garden-croft;
>   And gathering swallows twitter in the skies.

The opening line of this stanza has been condemned. Some critics have described these two questions as empty. How can you defend the line? What purpose does it serve?

P. The second stanza also begins with a question.

T. But that does not justify this one. What is the relation of this line to the remainder of the stanza?

P. It names the topic of the stanza.

T. That is true; but how would you justify the second question?

P. The second question is an echo of the first. It expresses Keats's enthusiasm, his delight.

P. It shows the ecstasy he feels as he thinks of the pleasures Autumn brings. Bare statements could not so well express his boundless joy.

T. As proof of this compare the following: On Tuesday, September 21 (1819) Keats wrote to Reynolds as follows:

How beautiful the season is now—how fine the air. A temperate sharpness about it. Really, without joking, chaste weather—Dian skies—I never lik'd stubble-fields so much as now—Aye better than the chilly green of the Spring. Somehow a stubble-plain looks warm—in the same way that some pictures look warm. This struck me so much in my Sunday's walk that I composed upon it.

At what time on a spring day are the "songs of Spring" most noticeable?

P. In the spring we notice the songs of birds in the early morning.

T. At what time of day did Keats hear the songs of Autumn?

P. He heard these sounds in the evening when the glow of the sunset was shed over everything—

> While barrèd clouds bloom the soft-dying day.

T. Why is this a better line than the original "While a gold cloud gilds the soft-dying day"?

P. "Gold" and "gilds" as image, sound, and colour are cold and hard—metallic; they have a limiting effect on the imagery. *Barrèd* and *bloom* suggest warmth and softness and changing colours.

P. The imagery in *barrèd* is clearer. The colour is better left to the imagination. *Bloom* suggests that both the colour and the contours of the sky are changing.

T. Read the remainder of the stanza aloud, giving slight emphasis to the words that hold some of the sound Keats heard.

P.

> Then in a *wailful* choir the small gnats *mourn*
>   *Among* the river sallows, *borne aloft*
>   Or sinking as the light wind *lives* or *dies*;

And full-grown lambs *loud bleat* from hilly *bourn*;
    Hedge-crickets *sing*; and now with treble soft
The redbreast *whistles* from a garden-croft;
    And gathering swallows *twitter* in the skies.

T. How would you describe the sound of this stanza?

P. It is soft and low. The sounds of Autumn might easily pass unnoticed by any but an attentive ear.

T. Keats compares the swarms of small insects to a choir. What are they supposed to mourn?

P. They mourn the day that is passing.

P. It may be that they are mourning the season that is drawing to its close.

T. The meaning and the imagery of this line are neither clear nor apt. It is probably the sound and the suggestion of these words that attracted Keats. Proof of this may be found in the word Keats coined for the line. *Wailful* reminds one of *easeful* in the lines from his *Ode to a Nightingale*:

> Darkling I listen; and, for many a time
>   I have been half in love with easeful Death.

By *wailful* Keats may have wished to suggest to us the drowsy effect of the low, continuous hum that fills the air on peaceful Autumn evenings. To Keats the hum caught in the sound of *wailful, mourn, among,* and *borne,* was not boringly monotonous. It was the characteristic chant of Autumn that formed a background for other choristers by hillside brooks, in garden plots, and in the skies, a background of bass for sopranos, altos, and tenors. How do the sounds heard in this stanza sustain the mood of drowsy and delightful satisfaction or "measureless content" created by the previous stanzas?

P. Because they are either faint, distantly vague, irregular, or slight, they intensify the silence and the peace of evening.

T. Each stanza deals with a different phase of one subject. How has the poet bound all three stanzas into a unity?

P. Throughout the poem, from the first line to the last, there is one mood. It is the poet's enthusiasm for Autumn, his feeling of delight, his ecstasy, that bind together not only lines but stanzas.

T. This feeling that we at first defined as a delight or an ecstasy we might now describe as an enchantment. The "full, close richness of the teeming earth" enchanted Keats, and he succeeded in imparting some of that enchantment to his poem. How he did this, may be discovered in his own advice to Shelley, a contemporary poet, "load every rift with ore". Once Keats was possessed by the mood, every image, sound, and rhythm had its apt significance. This evident enjoyment that Keats felt is still further intensified for us by the knowledge that Keats at the time of the composition of this poem knew that, owing to the rapid encroachment of "consumption", he would never know the peace and security that old age might bring, or the mellow ripeness of creative power perfectly controlled. Autumn for him was, nevertheless, not a time of death and decay, but a blessing, the delights of which he could imagine. It was for him a time of fulfilment, of consummation, of glorious achievement as permanent as his own poetic tribute. Bearing this in mind, let us have this "most Keatsian" poem read once again aloud.

P. (Reads.)

T. (1) If you wish to know more about the poetry and the life of Keats you may borrow from me these collections of his poems and his letters.

(2) If you wish to make for yourself a permanent record of your appreciation of this poem, make a written statement to support the following appraisal:

"In the autumn fields round Winchester, for the last time in this world his own free master, he found all his disciplined powers, of observation, of imagination, of craftsmanship, combining in one moment of power to produce the most serenely flawless poem in our language, *To Autumn.*"

(3) Find in *The Concise Oxford Dictionary* the definition of an ode, and after applying it to this poem explain why you think Keats entitled it *To Autumn* and not *Ode to Autumn*.

NOTES AND COMMENTS
ON THE TEACHING OF *To Autumn*

Briefly to remind the reader of some of the main ideas set forth in Chapter Two, may at this time give point and emphasis to the examination of the theory in the practice.

The teacher of English, it may be assumed, should know something of the process by which a work of literary art is created. He should understand something of the process by which imaginative experience is assimilated. He should regard his own function in the process of teaching to be like that of a creative artist who is trying by objective references to give concrete expression to subjective conditions. Sublimating his personal preferences, the teacher should regard both the materials of the poem and his method of teaching it as objectively as possible, aim to preserve the organic unity of the poem as a work of creative art, and keep the mind of the pupil preoccupied with the materials of the poem. If the teacher understands his job and can distinguish between skimming poetry and reading it, he will see to it that the poem does not pass across the pupil's mind, but rather that it passes into his mind as something possessing and finally to be possessed, as something not merely contemplated, but lived through. Endowed with a sense of perspective, proportion, orderliness, and restraint, he should be able to preserve the main sequence of the poem, analyzing, integrating, and synthesizing, as he proceeds. Forestalling fugitive speculation, he should aim to foster self-realization. The elements of the poem he will try to hold in solution until their precipitation begins to form in a cumulative effect. If he has the ability to interest others in what he deems worthy of interest, if he has the ability to win the confidence of the pupil and to awaken his intuitive powers, he may easily break down the pupil's natural resistance to mental activity and not only win his surrender to the mood and matter of the poem but also inspire him to reach, by a leap of sympathy from within, the spirit of the poem—perhaps even to discover for himself a new belief. He should be ready always to take advantage of every opportunity to further the pupil's appreciation of poetry by helping him to discover the steadying influence of a given image on the thought of a passage, the suggestiveness of a rhythm, the limiting effect of a given metre on the feeling, the stimulating effect on the imagination of an exotic comparison or figure of speech, the uniqueness of significant language, and the effect on substance of a given form. Not in analysis or in synthesis alone, but in the process of integrating all these various elements, is the pupil likely to discover poetry, and if in the process he puts forth freely all his powers at a stretch, learning to sublimate his instincts to the order imposed by the poem, and learning how to achieve a balance between the cold, calculating intellect and the warm, sympathetic intuition, he may in time feel the thrill of a quickened spirit and lay claim to poetic experience that is akin to the imaginative experience crystallized by the poet in the poem. Then, as Coleridge said, "You feel him to be a poet, inasmuch as for a time he has made you one—an active creative being."

The *reading* of poetry is a creative act. It is a process in which the reader, under the influence of the poem, gathers together the bare facts of his own imaginative experience and sets them forth, combined and integrated, in a new and significant order and form. It is a process in which the pursuit of a thing is more important than the thing pursued. With the poem *To Autumn* compare, for instance, a brief prose statement of its content, for example: The season of Autumn is marked by a superabundance of provisions, a languor of repletion, and a melody that is peculiarly its own. Or compare with the poem itself a collection of all the literary devices contained therein. Or again compare with the teaching of the poem a mere analysis of its content, and the difference between the pursuit of literary experience and the acquisition of literary knowledge should be abundantly clear.

In the teaching of the poem *To Autumn,* the following points in method have been illustrated.

(1) It is not always necessary to make some introductory comment before reading a poem to the class. Often the reading, either oral or silent, or both, is sufficient introduction to the study. If, however, an introduction is used, either to arouse interest or to supply helpful information, it should be brief and pertinent. It should lead directly to the poem and stop there. Let the poet work his spell!

To attempt to introduce this poem by asking questions such as "How do you feel in the Autumn?" "Why do you like the Autumn season?" or "What do you think of when Autumn is mentioned?" is to waste the time and the patience of the class. Such questions lead away from the poem. They encourage the pupil in the futile practice of self-indulgence and irresponsible self-expression. Likewise it is faulty practice to set the class a problem before reading the poem. Preoccupied with the task of finding a solution in the poem, the pupils miss everything else. Or suppose that the teacher, exhilarated by his own conceit, makes some personal subjective comment, by way of introduction, that leads the pupils to suspect that he is out of sympathy with the theme of the poem or the art of this particular poet. He is unfair to the pupil; he is standing in his own light. A good teacher would be more objective and impersonal in his attitude towards the class and his subject.

(2) Who should read the poem first? Invariably the pupil, or the teacher who is unprepared, reads just the words without their meanings. If, of course, an experienced pupil can prepare himself, there may be some defence for such a practice.

Whether the teacher reads to the class with books closed or open depends on the nature of the poem and the purpose for which it is being read. The choice here rests, as elsewhere in the teaching of poetry, on the judgment, good taste, and commonsense of the teacher.

(3) To discover the significance of any detail or part of a poem, one must examine it in the light of the poem as a whole. The purpose of the first question after the completion of the reading is to secure the contemplation of the whole poem by the whole class. This silent reading by the class is, in the treatment of some poems, one of the most valuable steps in the whole lesson, provided, of course, that the attention of the pupils is concentrated on the discovery of the central mood or image or thought or whatever may constitute the main theme of the poem. The attempt to identify and name this idea or emotion affords the pupils excellent practice in both comprehension and composition.

(4) The reader should observe at what point the particular or detailed analysis of the poem begins.

(5) The study of the poem should follow the sequence laid down by the poet. A question or a comment thrown out at random to fall anywhere within the limits of the poem may, for the moment, give the teacher the prestige of feigned omniscience, but in the end it confuses and disconcerts the pupil. How often in classroom or lecture-

hall the instructor in English pauses at, let us say, line 20 to make some comment the value of which is lost because the student has been unable to take the preliminary steps that led the instructor to that peak of insight! This kind of "hit and miss" questioning (or comment) leads to analysis without the accompanying synthesis and integration—that is, to analysis for the sake of analysis, or to comment for the sake of sententiousness. The result is fugitive speculation, not training in self-control and self-realization. Questions should be aimed to make each element of the poetry that contributes to the unity of the poem reveal its significance when it occurs and always with its immediate context in mind. Since the colour, sound, connotation, quality, or position of a word is often more important in poetry than its meaning, the teacher whenever possible should draw attention to the significance of the word *to* its context, as well as to its meaning *in* its context. An acceptance of this belief might eliminate forever the practice, still too common, of assigning a class for homework the task of securing the dictionary meanings of words selected from the next day's lesson. At all costs the teacher should preserve the unity of the poem as a work of art and take everything that is of value to the sequence as he proceeds, so long as he does not break the canons of artistic restraint or sacrifice the confidence and co-operation of the class. He should link together the various elements of the poetry within the poem, and not lap the poem several times to find its poetic ingredients. A recipe is not a cake; a seed catalogue is not a garden; a collection of literary devices is not a poem; and a group of responses to literary stimuli, despite all that I. A. Richards has written, is not a guarantee of poetic experience. If an image or a rhythm or a metaphor is significant, find out at once when it occurs, what it contributes to its context, and how it sustains the effect being produced. Direct attention to the effect of the device rather than to the device or its name. A pupil may discover a comparison and identify it, perhaps correctly, as a simile, but his knowledge and skill avail him little unless he discovers what the comparison, where it occurs, contributes to the clarity of an image, the heightening of a thought, or the deepening of an emotion. The questions themselves, moreover, should be in logical sequence and lead to clearly defined and useful ends.

(6) As the study of the poem proceeds, either the teacher or a pupil reads again the passage about to be discussed. This practice helps to preserve the continuity of thought and feeling, to keep the attention of the class concentrated on the material, to bring out the rhythmic effects of the passage, and to establish an interest, perhaps a delight, in the careful utterance of memorable speech.

(7) Once the pupil is on the track of the poet, he is quick in pursuit. This belief is a defence for the sudden shift of leadership from the teacher to the pupil in the middle of the first stanza. In the teaching of *To Autumn* explanations by the teacher are longer and more frequent than they are in the study of later poems. Eventually a well-trained class that knows how to "read" poetry will move quickly and surely to the discovery and assimilation of poetic experience.

(8) Near the beginning of the study the attention of the class is directed to Keats's use of compound words. It

is unwise for the teacher to harp on this subject every time thereafter that a compound word is encountered. But the pupil should not be restrained from doing so if he can show what is gained by its use. In fact, the teacher should encourage the pupil to make discoveries within the limits of the passage under discussion. Whenever he perceives that the pupil is about to take wing, he should quickly step aside and await the result, insisting only that the fledgling finds a safe perch for his feet at the end of his flight and is not driven about by the merciless gusts of wanton fancy. This, by the way, is one of the more important values of literary study, i.e. to give the pupil practice in directing his powers of thinking, feeling, and imagining to given worthy ends.

(9) When recapitulating the material of a stanza at the end of its study, care should be taken to use only those facts and conditions that have been discovered in the process of teaching. Too often teachers are heard to introduce ideas or comments which in themselves may have merit, but which, for the pupil, lack validity, because he cannot see how they were deduced.

(10) This does not apply to quotations or illustrations used to awaken thought or imagination. Sometimes other versions of the same material can be used effectively to develop literary taste. Often a dull variant, invented by the teacher and offered in place of the poet's word in its poetic context, will bring to light all the brilliance and significance of the poet's word. Contrasts help to clarify ideas and images, just as contrasts in rhyming sounds (for example -ness, sun, bless, run, etc.) deepen the harmony and increase the musical effect of all that surrounds them.

(11) Most things, be they persons or poems, that are placed on a pedestal are usually left "on the shelf". Pupils are only too skilful at paying feigned deference to their aloof positions, and pass blithely along without them. If poetic experience is to mean anything in the life of the pupil, he must meet it at his own level, and then rise with it, or better, through it. What defence is there for professionalism? It is founded in either conceit or bluff. Its aim is tyranny. In its presence poetic experience cannot be found.

(12) In conclusion of the study a good test of what the pupils have made of a poem is found in their oral reading of it. Sometimes an original, written statement of the poet's success in blending substance and form will serve as well. Comparisons, however, are usually not worth the time it takes to make them. If they are used, the poems should be chosen for their similarity of mood rather than their similarity of subject or of form. The advocates of the extensive study of poetry recommend the cursory reading of a number of poems on the same subject in preference to the intensive study of one. From this kind of practice the really able pupils turn away in disgust, and the less able carry away a mistaken notion of the nature and value of poetry. When two sonnet forms are compared, it is form and not poetry that is considered, and form is only one of the many elements in poetry. If poetic moods are to be compared, then both poems will require very careful study. One poem that has entered into a pupil's being and has evoked his creative power to meet it, is worth more than a dozen poems that have passed, no matter how colourfully or musically, across his

placid consciousness. It is just the difference that exists between an artist's contemplation of a scene and a motorist's fleeting glance across a landscape.

Parodies, too, must be used with great discretion. They may imitate some of the words or the form of the original, but they express a meaning that has little to do with the original. Like clowns, they may serve useful purposes if both time and place are well chosen. Otherwise they offend against the laws of decency and good taste.

There is, however, no formal method of teaching literature. Every teacher must develop and pursue his own method, but the best of possible methods is worthless unless the principles on which it is founded are sound and the teacher who practises it has to some degree insight, initiative, and good judgment. An unsympathetic reader, who does not care to distinguish between mere interrogation of a pupil and systematic questioning on a poem, will see little more in this lesson, *To Autumn,* than a string of questions and answers. The more sympathetic readers will perceive in it a method in which the art of the poem may manifest itself, a ritual in which the spirit of the pupil may meet in imagination the spirit of the poetry. A poem is a work of literary art; the teaching of poetry may also be an art.

'Twixt Theory and Practice

No one who has really entered into the poem, *To Autumn,* who has surrendered himself to it and has lived through the creative process of making up a new experience within his own mind, supported by the convictions of his own thinking, feeling, and imagining, and guided by the teacher's vision and the teaching ritual; no one who has thus achieved an experience akin to the poet's original experience, as crystallized in the poem, will deny that this poem possesses a spirit of its own—a power to awaken his intuition, deepen his insight, purge his feelings by sublimation, and influence his imagination. The purpose of either of the problems given at the end of the study of the poem is to intensify further the pupil's contemplation of the whole experience as discovered in the form and substance of the poem.

The spirit of poetry, when really encountered, quickens the spirit of the reader. This attribute of poetry is often referred to as its inspirational power. It is the power latent in genuine poetry to lift up the mind of the reader *within* reality, the power to help him to discover the ideal *within* the real, and not outside it. It is the power to find in commonplace things a significance that is aesthetic and often spiritual. It works like magic. Autumn for a reader who has once laid claim to a poetic experience akin to that of Keats, is a memorable autumn. The reader has encountered the spirit, the very essence, of the season, and his insight and vision are sharpened and clarified in the process. He will no longer be able to behold the autumn landscape as a commonplace. Henceforth the season of autumn will be something to contemplate because he was once in communion with its spirit. Poetic experience, like real experience, when fully assimilated, changes the reader. Properly guided, it exercises a mighty influence on the shaping of character because it not only increases the reader's outlook, perspective, and horizon, but also awakens and directs to worthy ends all his creative instincts and powers.

I have said that poetry interprets in two ways; it interprets by expressing with magical felicity the physiognomy and movement of the outward world, and it interprets by expressing, with inspired conviction, the ideas and laws of the inward world of man's moral and spiritual nature. In other words, poetry is interpretative both by having *natural magic* in it, and by having *moral profundity*. In both ways it illuminates man; it gives him a satisfying sense of reality; it reconciles him with himself and the universe.[1]

And Matthew Arnold might have added that it releases powers pent up within the reader, instincts and energies, which when sublimated and refined in the creative process of making a new integration, unify the whole personality of the reader and temper his spirit. The exalted *self* in the individual is lost, to be found again in the dignity of humility. The individual, who alone has the power to act intelligently, acts with more wisdom and greater vision towards nobler ends. And on the training of character to these ends, rests today the foundations of our survival as a people. It is not autumn, the season, that we memorialize here, but rather the power of inspiration, latent in genuine poetry, to lead us to see into ourselves and into the very heart of things. Real and imaginative experience enhance each other.

If man is the only creature capable of intelligent action, it is paramount that we concern ourselves with the kind of man who is going to take action. It is not enough that he be a man of intellect; he must be a man of intelligence. It is not enough that he be a man of ability; he must be a man of quality. It is not enough that he be a man of much learning; he must be a man of good taste, and

[1] Matthew Arnold, *Maurice de Guérin*.

sound judgment, and common sense. Unless a man of much scholarship is also a man of sound character, his knowledge merely emphasizes his hollowness.

Consequently when the teacher has evidence of the pupil's ability to identify a central thought, feeling, or image; to point out the unusual significance or application of words; to give reasons for preferring a given order, rhythm, or sound; to explain the successful or unsuccessful blending of matter, form, and style; or to show what an apt figure contributes to the clarity or intensity of a thought, feeling, or image, he should not be misled into believing that this kind of literary appreciation is identical with poetic experience or proof of its existence. The method by which a thing is sought must not be confused with the thing itself. Likewise the teacher must not suppose that when he has set before the pupil standards of experience worthy of response, has secured his concentrated attention, has subjected him to disciplined thinking and feeling, has helped him to make a finer adjustment to life, has encouraged him in the discovery of new beliefs, and has revealed to him the charm of language gracefully controlled, he must not suppose that when he has done all these things he has conditioned both the course and the destination of the pupil's mind. Poetic experience matures as the result of a process. It is not a delayed response, but a cumulative effect. Unlike the method, it is highly personal and subjective, and it is precisely in this quality that it can have any social value. The social order will continue to be a pale reflection of the philosophy of *laissez-faire,* the fashion of complacency, and the habit of wishful thinking, unless the fundamental precepts and values of science, art, and religion are inculcated on the minds and hearts of our people.

> Plain living and high thinking are no more:
> The homely beauty of the good old cause
> Is gone; our peace, our fearful innocence
> And pure religion breathing household laws.[1]

The ideal of sober virtues that we seek will not result from the subtle manipulation or propagandizing of groups of humanity. It can be reached only through the regeneration of the individual. In this process great art, and especially poetry, has its part to play. But there must be less skimming of poems for aesthetic enjoyment, and more reading or teaching of poetry and surrender to its spirit. When the surrender is complete, the reader feels the impact of the spirit with which great art is divinely inspired.

Reading may be one of life's inexhaustible pleasures and blessings, but may also become a mere habit, an escape from thinking, or a drug.[2]

Properly taught, however, poetry can work wonders in shaping individual character and, through the individual, in moulding the ideals of a whole people. Behold the legacy we have received from Shakespeare. As teachers of poetry our duty is plain and our responsibility inescapable. What hope is there for a people when they forget their mystics and their poets?

[1] William Wordsworth, *September 1802*.
[2] Walter de la Mare, *Early One Morning in the Spring*. Faber.

Chapter Four

ON FIRST LOOKING INTO CHAPMAN'S HOMER

POETS often turn for guidance and inspiration to the works of their predecessors. Keats, for instance, turned to Shakespeare and Milton, Chaucer and Spenser, and found both recreation and inspiration in their poetry. Keats, moreover, with his friend Charles Cowden Clarke, found profit in reading together Pope's translation of Homer's *Odyssey* (published about 1730). The bond of friendship between these two young men was literature in general and poetry in particular. They read together what they described as "the finest passages".

One day in October of 1816 (Keats only 21) Clarke met Keats and invited him to his house in London to read with him that night parts of Chapman's translation of Homer's *Odyssey* (published in 1614). Clarke had borrowed it from Mr. Alsager (financial department of the London *Times*). They read together "the famousest passages" and as Clarke read he looked up at times to be greeted by one of Keats's "delighted stares". They read and discussed through the night, and early in the morning Keats left for his home two miles away. Clarke went to bed. Next morning when Clarke came down at 10 A.M. he found on his library table a letter addressed to himself in the handwriting of Keats. He opened it and read— *On First Looking into Chapman's Homer.*

T. (Reads the poem.)

> Much have I travell'd in the realms of gold,
> And many goodly states and kingdoms seen;
> Round many western islands have I been
> Which bards in fealty to Apollo hold.
> Oft of one wide expanse had I been told
> That deep-brow'd Homer ruled as his demesne:
> Yet did I never breathe its pure serene
> Till I heard Chapman speak out loud and bold:
> Then felt I like some watcher of the skies
> When a new planet swims into his ken;
> Or like stout Cortez, when with eagle eyes
> He stared at the Pacific—and all his men
> Look'd at each other with a wild surmise—
> Silent, upon a peak in Darien.

This letter contained no mention of the obvious "Thanks for a pleasant evening"; yet it expressed the fine delight which had been Keats's the night before—the essence of his ecstasy compressed into a work of immortal art.

T. To what does Keats compare himself in the opening line?

P. To a traveller.[1]

T. (Reads first four lines.)

> Much have I travell'd in the realms of gold,
> And many goodly states and kingdoms seen;
> Round many western islands have I been
> Which bards in fealty to Apollo hold.

T. What were the fields of his explorations?

P. "Realms of gold", "goodly states", "kingdoms", "western islands".

T. These are all vague, romantic words, suggestive of associations of the past.

---

[1] In this lesson many of the answers are not given in the form of complete statements. If the sense is complete, why make a fetish of pedagogy and a parrot of the pupil?

T. Who is the lord in these territories?

P. Apollo.

T. Who is Apollo?

P. God of the sun.

T. Yes, of light—hence of literature—patron saint of music and poetry.

T. Who pay allegiance to him?

P. The bards.

T. What is the nature of that allegiance as implied in fealty (*fidelitas*)?

P. The allegiance of vassals to a lord.

T. What, then, are the realms of gold if they are not the *eldorado* of Spanish conquerors?

P. The realms of literature—the masterpieces of the past: as seen in his reading and imagination.

T. What literature in particular?

P. Greek—perhaps Roman too.

T. Then he says "western islands". Where are these?

P. The British Isles.

T. Further he mentions "kingdoms"—if kingdoms then kings. Who are some of the kings of literature to whom he has paid allegiance?

P. Shakespeare, Spenser, Pope, Milton, Chaucer, etc.

T. Poets often use emotional words to show their private feelings concerning their subject-matter. Which word here lets us into the poet's mind?

P. "Goodly".

T.

> Oft of one wide expanse had I been told
>> That deep-browed Homer ruled as his demesne:
>> Yet did I never breathe its pure serene
> Till I heard Chapman speak out loud and bold:

T. Keats says he has travelled in "realms of gold" and now he implies that in his travels he has been told of another realm in particular. What words does he use to name it?

P. "Wide expanse".

T. Which of these words carries his personal feelings as he views this land in imagination?

P. "Wide", and by this he suggests that it is spacious and full of wonders.

T. Who is the ruler here?

P. Homer.

T. What does the epithet "deep-browed" betoken?

P. Large intelligence, understanding, *wisdom*.

T. Where had he discovered this *leader's* demesne?

P. In Pope's translation of Homer's *Odyssey*. He found it described there.

T.

> Yet did I never breathe its pure serene
> Till I heard Chapman speak out loud and bold:

T. Which words tell us that he found in Chapman a better translation—one that appealed to Keats?

P. "Loud" and "bold".

T. There may be an implied contrast here between the elegant, artificial language of Pope's age and the *force* and *rapidity* of movement in Chapman's metrical translation. Chapman spoke out *loud* and *bold*: He had caught and transmitted some of Homer's power. What was the first effect on Keats? In the first version of the poem, the one that Clarke read on that October morning in 1816 at 10 A.M. this line ran "Yet did I never judge what men might mean". Contrast this with the second version "Yet did I never breathe its pure serene". Why is the second version the better one?

PP. (*A composite answer.*) *Judge* implies intellectual appraisal—criticism of Homer through Pope and others; *breathe* implies a physical or emotional response. The pure, clear air of that wide expanse gave him a new lease on life—stimulation and inspiration.

T.

> Then felt I like some watcher of the skies
> When a new planet swims into his ken;

"Then felt I"—Here is an indication that the direction of the thought is changed. What change do you notice?

PP. (*A composite answer.*) The first eight lines have been *expository,* and these statements have been with the exception of *loud and bold* couched in vague and abstract language which conveys more by suggestion and romantic association than it does by direct statement. Now the thought turns inward and the words record the poet's personal feelings or response. Not what I have *seen* or *heard* but what I have *felt* is now uppermost in the mind of Keats.

T. To what does he compare himself?

P. To a watcher, an astronomer.

T. To what does he compare his thrill of discovery in Chapman's Homer?

P. To that of an astronomer who plots and discovers a new star or planet in the heavens—a new planet swims into his line of vision.

T. It is interesting at this point to remember that Keats won a prize on leaving school. It was a gift of Bonny-castle's *Introduction to Astronomy* and we are told that a chapter in that book, which dealt with Astronomy and Discovery made a great impression on Keats. Doubtless he recalled it as he walked home from Clarke's in the fading star-light of that early dawn. The comparison rose easily to his mind and seemed appropriate and good—he accepted it. How does it sustain or develop the implied comparison which was introduced in the first line of the poem?

P. Both the traveller in imagination and this watcher made discoveries.

T.

> Or like stout Cortez when with eagle eyes
>   He stared at the Pacific—and all his men
> Looked at each other with a wild surmise—
>   Silent, upon a peak in Darien.

To what does the poet now compare himself?

P. To Cortez, the founder of Mexico—one of the famous conquistadors of the sixteenth century.

T. It was really Balboa, a Spanish adventurer, who in September 1513 was the first white man to see the Pacific Ocean from a mountain top in the Isthmus of Panama, or Darien, but Keats chose Cortez, perhaps because Titian's portrait of Cortez, which he had seen earlier with Leigh Hunt, was with its "eagle eyes" as Keats remarked to Hunt, still dominating his mind. Cortez meant something to him. This plus the following passage from Robertson's *History of America* (a book that interested Keats at school) provided the material for this second simile or comparison.

At length the Indians assured them, that from the top of the next mountain they should discover the ocean which was the object of their wishes. When, with infinite toil, they had climbed up the greater part of that steep ascent, Balboa commanded his men to halt, and advanced alone to the summit, that he might be the first who should enjoy a spectacle which he had so long desired. As soon as he beheld the South Sea stretching in endless prospect below him, he fell on his knees, and lifting up his hands to Heaven, returned thanks to God. . . . His followers, observing his transports of joy, rushed forward to join in his wonder, exultation and gratitude.

This plus the passage interpolated between dashes in the poem, gives the reader some idea of the relative positions of the leader and his men on that mountain top as Keats views the scene in imagination.

T. On what does it fix the reader's attention?

*P. Cortez—eagle eyes—stared—silent—*upon *a peak in Darien.*

T. How does Keats sustain and reinforce the element of wonder?

P.

> —and all his men
> Looked at each other with a wild surmise—

T. Of the last line "Silent, upon a peak in Darien", Leigh Hunt once wrote "We leave the reader standing upon it with all the illimitable world of thought and feeling before him, to which his imagination will have brought him, while journeying through these 'realms of gold'." Great poets working in the white heat of creation when thought, feeling, imagination are all fused in rhythm and form, do not waste energy in repetition. The sestet, or last six lines of this poem, consists of two comparisons, two similes; the second does not surely repeat the first. What is common to them?

P. Both sustain the original idea of a voyage of discovery.

T. How can one distinguish between them?

PP. (*A composite answer.*) The first presents the image of a man who stays at home and who, with his telescope, makes discoveries in the regions beyond this planet. The second presents the image of a man who actually goes out to make discoveries for himself. The second comparison continues and surpasses the first. Keats, when he read Chapman, felt not only the thrill of discovery that an astronomer might feel, but he, like the *stout* Cortez, felt in his whole being the stimulation of that rare atmosphere on the mountain peak in Darien. He felt that he was actually in the world of the Odyssey.

T. Similes and metaphors are not mere literary devices introduced into poetry to provide decorative ornament. They are part of the texture of thought and feeling. They fertilize and stimulate the thought and feeling of the reader. How do these similes or comparisons enhance the thought, feeling, and beauty of this poem?

P. 1. They make the ideas and suggestions in the octave and the associations attached to the words of the octave more concrete by giving the imagination definite images to stand upon.

2. They lift the emotional tone of the poem to a higher pitch.

T. What words by their sounds or suggestions sustain this upward inflection?

P. Eagle eyes — wild surmise — silent — peak — Darien (compare the effect of a peak in Panama).

T. These comparisons contain the living spirit of discovery. With the opening words "Then felt I" the poet's thoughts and feelings turned first inward and then through his imagination upward until he found himself on a hitherto undiscovered peak of experience. What effect then had the reading of Chapman's Homer upon Keats?

P. 1. It inspired him to great poetic achievement. This poem was written in 1816: Keats' great year, the spring of 1818 to the spring of 1819, was yet to come.

2. It gave him a glimpse of a new world of beauty and wonder.

T. Read the poem aloud. (*One of the pupils reads.*)

Notes and Comments on the Teaching of
On First Looking into Chapman's Homer

As mentioned earlier, all poems do not need special introductions. If, however, an introduction is deemed necessary or appropriate, it should be an introduction and not a preface or a preamble. It should lead at once to the study of the poem and make the approach to its central theme immediate and direct.

The medium of poetry is *words*. If their order and quality are to be appreciated, words must be left in their contexts. There, they are alive! The meaning of the word *fealty*, for instance, offers little difficulty if left in its context by the question "What is the nature of this allegiance as implied in *fealty*?"

Once the predominant idea or image or mood is identified, pursue it through the logical sequence of the poem by giving appropriate emphasis to the concrete details by which it is sustained. In this poem the predominent image is that of a traveller. Keats saw himself as a traveller in imagination. This image is still supporting him in the last line where he stands

> Silent upon a peak in Darien.

If the teacher fails to see this, he belabours the poem with questions and comments, and the poem disintegrates in his hands. Such an exhaustive treatment exhausts the class, and it would have been better if the poem had merely been read and summarily dismissed.

In preparing to teach a poem, let the teacher try to make a brief statement of its central theme in his own words for his own guidance.

Something like the following is a safe *first* step to take in the preparation of this lesson.

(In the poem *On First Looking into Chapman's Homer*, Keats shows the effect that the reading of parts of Chapman's translation of Homer had upon his mind and spirit. As a reader Keats compares himself to a traveller—a sailor exploring strange lands and far seas that are the literary masterpieces of past ages. This comparison is maintained throughout the whole poem, and the consistency of all the details with this image adds to the unity of this sonnet as a work of art. The charm of the poem, however, derives from the aptness and the suggestiveness of the two comparisons that comprise the sestet. In the connotation or sound or imagery of the words *eagle eyes, stared, wild surmise, silent, Darien,* the poet has caught the elusive spirit that keeps literature alive. By means of these words and images the reader glimpses the magic and senses the wonder that give literature the power to bear him away in imagination to islands beyond his real experience, to realms of gold hitherto unknown.)

Many teachers, however, will feel no need for such a humdrum performance, but it is to be hoped that should they miss the poetry, they will not rely on the collecting of literary devices and pretend that they are teaching poetry. Devices are means to an end, but they are not to be regarded as ends in themselves. It is the effect of a device that is unique. The image of the traveller or explorer helps to *steady* the thought and feeling running through the poem, in much the same way as the keel helps to keep a ship on its course. The two similes with which the sonnet closes turn the thought and feeling into unexplored channels of haunting wonder. They are evidence of the urgency and intensity of the poet's imagination. They are also causes of stimulation of the reader's emotions and fertilization of his thinking.

A teacher who lacks an imaginative grasp of any unit of work that he is trying to teach is not likely to meet with success. He labours wearily over all the details without seeing their interrelation or the ends to which they lead. To him facts are as uninteresting and unprovocative as boulders strewn over an untravelled plateau. Surely all facts and details are not of equal value! Surely some of them should be grouped to a climax! If the teacher will aim at the half dozen mountain peaks of interest and value in a lesson, the valleys will take care of themselves. In print, of course, it is almost impossible to reflect the spontaneity of either the teacher or the pupil when a pinnacle of discovery in a lesson is reached. Print runs at the pace of the eye; speech flies with the rush of emotion or rests in the silence of the imagination. The possibilities for variety are infinite if the principles of the method are sound. Perhaps it is in a well-calculated teaching ritual that the spirit finds support for its wings.

There are a few novices teaching English who regard method as a restriction upon their personal liberty. For them literary analysis is a sacrilege—an offence against what they call beauty. They demand freedom—breathing space—in which to hold forth on the poet's life, his style, critics' opinions of his work, or their own appreciation of poetry. Sometimes their conception of a lesson in literature descends to the level of a radio book review. They wish to impress the pupil, to create "literary atmosphere", but not to teach him. They fail to see that without the restraint of form the substance of this sonnet would still be unknown. Genuine freedom is not a product of humanistic self-indulgence or self-expression. It is an adjunct to order and discipline, not the littered residue of chaos. If there is anything in the teacher's character or personality that is worth transmitting, it will become entangled with the subject he teaches. Like the spirit of poetry, it illuminates the order it inhabits.

An imaginative teacher who has an insight into the nature of poetry will preserve the unity of substance and form as inseparable parts of a poem. A sonnet is not a sonnet because of its form alone. It has, of course, a special rhythm and rhyme scheme, but it also has a very special sonnet point of view. It is a thought or a mood or an image of a particular kind and quality. It is absurd in the study of a sonnet as literature to treat the octave and the sestet as separable parts of the poem. They depend on each other. The thought or feeling in the observations of the octave reach their climax in the reflections of the sestet. They may change in direction as they proceed, but their means of conveyance remains the same from beginning to end for the express purpose of reaching that end with all their baggage.

Keep the attention of the class concentrated on the discovery of poetry, and the poem with all its elements interrelated will retain the unity of a work of art. Win the surrender of the pupil to poetry; lead him to project himself, through the ritual of your method, into its spirit; deepen his personal subjective encounter with it, his reflection upon it, and his response to it, by subjecting the work of art to an impersonal objective inquiry; guarantee to the pupil freedom of spirit by helping him to clear away all physical and mental obstacles; at all costs distinguish between genuine freedom that, through method and disciplined thinking and feeling, prepares the way for the attainment of a new peak of experience and that other "freedom", the spurious artificial freedom of the false liberator who would lead us into a broad waste of superficiality in order to attain mediocrity!

Keats' famous sonnet *On First Looking into Chapman's Homer* can stand alone today as it has stood for over one hundred years and as it will remain for centuries to come, a masterpiece among English sonnets. To set it off, it does not need either a prologue such as Hardy's *When I Set Out for Lyonnesse* or an epilogue such as Andrew Lang's *The Odyssey*. Its sublimity is untouched by comparisons. The human mind does well to contemplate one thing at a time. Comparisons, unless the poetic experiences of both poems have been separately apprehended, are likely to be more confusing than illuminating.

Chapter Five

THE QUESTION OF QUESTIONING

The true approach to knowledge was not through books or
lectures, but through conversation, discussion, question and answer,
two or more persons beating a subject up and down, till the chaff
is winnowed from the wheat . . . [1]

Good questioning is one of the most important sources
of good teaching. Poor questioning is worse than talking
at a class. One of the secrets of good questioning is found
in good preparation and lesson planning. Unless the
teacher knows at least some of the answers that lead to a
well-defined climax in a lesson, he will hardly be able to
question with clarity and sequence of thought. Clear
questioning is a product of clear thinking. A teacher
who, for instance, has only a misty view of the horizon to
which a poem leads cannot question intelligently on the
subject. He proceeds to talk vaguely about it.

Good questioning is usually a sign of mental prowess
and leadership; sometimes it is the means by which a
teacher's resourcefulness is revealed. When, for instance,
one of his "key" questions fails to open the door to
knowledge or experience, the resourceful teacher proceeds
to pick the lock. Less agile minds would begin to splutter
and give themselves away.

But let us examine a few questions to see how they
may be improved.

[1] Sir Richard Livingstone, *Portrait of Socrates.* Oxford.

1. Who dragged whom around the walls of what?

This question contains three of the mental can-openers
—who, whom, what, where, when, why, how, etc., but it
seeks too many facts "at one fell swoop". It may startle
the pupil, but it fails to stimulate his mind or to win his
respectful response.

2. What *about* the alliteration in this line? (It alliter-
ates.) What *about* the interest in this paragraph? (It
interests.) How *about* the people during the industrial
revolution? (Not all industrious.) What do you think
about Europe? (Well, what about it?) What do you
think *about* Hamlet's killing of Polonius? (It was a good
idea.)

The periphrastic *about* in questioning often leads to
vague thinking. It is usually a sign that the teacher does
not know what he wants. Sometimes it leads to the smart
answer that in turn may lead the pupil down that cir-
cuitous escape to the principal's office to explain his
insolence. Nearly all breaches of discipline can be traced
to breaches in the teacher's thinking or preparation. What
is the purpose of the alliteration? or, What contributes
to the interest? or, Why does the paragraph interest you?
Any of these questions will give some direction and challenge to the pupil, and this the *about* questions usually
fail to do.

3. What about Macduff—how does he compare with
these people?

The person who asked this question began to speak
before he began to think, and continued speaking after he
had stopped thinking. "What about Macduff—" is a
mental breather; and "with these people" is a sign of

fatigue. What comparison can be made between Macduff and Banquo as patriots? is clear, brief, direct, and answerable.

4. The characteristics of Macbeth are what? or The characteristics of Macbeth are ... ?

The questioner at first intended to name the characteristics of Macbeth, but suddenly (in the first example) bethought himself of his prerogative and exclaimed "are what?" or (in the second example) waited in breathless suspense for the pupil to complete the question for him. Both questions are partly declarative and partly interrogative in form. It would have been more logical to make it a question throughout—What are the characteristics of Macbeth? To reverse the gears in forward-moving thought is most unsettling.

5. Macbeth was suspicious of Banquo, was he not?

Here is a similar mistake in form, but this time the question is answerable by yes or no. The pupil feels no provocation to think because the teacher has done the thinking for him. Why was Macbeth suspicious of Banquo? would have challenged the pupil.

6. Shylock shows how cunning he is here, don't you think so?

This is another variety of the same form, but this time the teacher, instead of arousing interest, argument, and discussion, invites complete agreement. This is the beginning of a form of patronage that insults the intelligence of a class. Ask simply, How does Shylock show his cunning?

7. Do you think that is a good comparison there?

This leads nowhere. It is a signal of distress. It wastes time. What are the points of comparison? is surely an improvement on this question!

8. What does this word mean? or What do you think is meant by this word?

Questions of this type force words out of their contexts, and when they are used continuously in a lesson they destroy interest not only by monotony, but also by failure to penetrate the substance of literature. Meaning is not the only significance that a word may have.

9. How many know the significance of this word?

What the teacher really wishes to know is not *How many know?* but *What is the significance of this word?*

10. Brown, do you like this poem?

The weaknesses of this question are so obvious that a better form should by comparison condemn its use. Why do you like this poem, (pause) Brown?

11. A *leading* question gives the pupil a clue to the answer expected. A *key* question opens up a problem just as a loosened key-log releases a log-jam. Leading questions should be used with discretion. Key questions are common and sometimes numerous in a lesson; and each one is usually followed by a series of derived questions in sequence. The pupil's answer should lead to the next question.

12. Tell all you know about the rhythm of this poem. Or, Discuss the stanza form of this poem.

These statements fail to provide the pupil with any direction for answering. Anything he offers must be accepted. They do not place on the pupil any responsibility for an organized answer, and they provide him with neither a lead nor a key to what is required.

13. What must a poet have before he can write a poem?

Such questions, asked probably in all seriousness, may sound very silly when delivered. Despite anything sensible that might be said in answer to this question, I should think that a silly answer, "A pint of beer", or "A punch below the belt" would perhaps contain more truth; but I am quite sure that I should be thrown out of some classrooms for offering it.

14. The questioning is faulty if the questions are too long or involved to be followed easily. This fault can be corrected by presenting the problem in a few clear statements, and then by driving a short, sharp, thought-provoking question into the heart of the problem.

15. A long series of short, fact-finding questions delivered with the rapid-fire of a machine-gun, is sometimes a sign that the teacher is not well prepared to teach. Even in a review lesson or a recitation lesson material should be gathered into problem-questions that arouse interest and stimulate thought.

16. The questioning is faulty if the teacher must be constantly rewording or reframing his thought. This fault disappears when the teacher is well prepared to teach the lesson and can judge the ability of his pupils.

17. The questioning is faulty if no distinction is made between a group of questions addressed to the whole class, but answered by one pupil, and a group of separate questions answered by different pupils. Pupils often learn

more from one another than they do from the teacher. It is easier for them to follow the thought through a series of answers from one pupil dealing with an isolated point in preparation for some larger problem than to follow the answers all over the room.

The following series of questions might be answered by one pupil:

How many accented syllables are there in this line?

How many unaccented syllables?

What is the metre?

18. Between questions that seek facts and those that seek the relationship of facts or facts in their relationships, a distinction is usually made in form, delivery, and fixity of assignment. All questions, however, should challenge the concentrated effort of the whole class.

19. The questioning is faulty if the teacher asks a question and then proceeds to talk against the pupil's desire to think it out or to answer it. Usually by the time the teacher has finished talking, he has forgotten the original question, and the pupil has lost all desire to answer it. This is one of the quickest and surest ways to lose the goodwill and co-operation of a class. Observe yourself to see what a temptation it is; observe others to see how devastating is the effect upon your interest. Distinction, however, must be made between this type of procedure and that in which the teacher uses a topical question to draw attention to a subject that he is going to explain.

20. A lesson should not be a series of alternate short questions and answers. Both teacher and pupils

frequently expand answers and by their remarks help to preserve the continuity and to deepen the intensity of thought and feeling in a lesson.

21. The attitude of a good questioner is one of sympathy, courtesy, toleration, tact, and eagerness to learn from others; it should never be that of a cross-examiner. The teacher is one of the group he teaches, and, like his pupils, should be a learner too. His questions, however, should give clear, definite, and efficient leadership to thought.

22. Questioning should never be an end in itself. It should be a means to develop the subject, pursue a logical sequence, and train pupils in efficient habits of study.

23. The proper organization and spacing of questions depends on the teacher's perspective on the subject, on his ability to distinguish between peaks and valleys of interest, between what is important and what is only essential, and on his sense of proportion and restraint.

24. A good questioner frequently refers his pupils to the process by which the subject is being developed in order that they may see for themselves the progress being made—the direction whence they have come and whither they are going. It is a good plan, from time to time, to invite them to ask the questions, i.e. to select the material on which a question is to be placed and then to frame the question best suited to draw the response required. An able senior pupil might well be entrusted from time to time with the teaching of some lessons or parts of lessons, under the supervision of the teacher. One danger of allowing just anyone in the class to ask the questions is that the whole procedure becomes unwieldy and confused.

25. The teacher must, of course, first *learn the lesson* he is going to teach; then he must *learn how to teach it*. When he is fully prepared, his time in class will not be so preoccupied with the subject that he is unable to study, direct, and guide judiciously the responses of his pupils. The making of questions is a fine skill; the guiding of responses is a fine art.

ON RECEIVING ANSWERS

In a lesson on Scott's *Rosabelle* the following procedure was once observed.

T. Why does Rosabelle wish to go to Roslin?

P. She wants to be at the ball.

T. I think she does, too.

It is obvious to everyone that the teacher's agreement with the pupil added little to this discussion. It was irrelevant! The fact that the pupil's answer was incomplete was apparently not considered worthy of attention.

The method of questioning may reveal the teacher's technical skill, resourcefulness, and powers of leadership. The manner in which he receives answers and deals with them may reveal his character, i.e. the kind of person he is. If he is lazy, indifferent, intolerant, unsympathetic, tactless, or patronizing, he will soon reveal his weakness in his attitude to his pupils and his job. If his standards of achievement, taste, or decency are low, his pupils will soon discover it. Good classroom procedure is one of the best of all illustrations of practical democracy at work. The pupil should not get the impression that he is answering to please himself alone, to please the teacher alone, or to show how cleverly he can guess what the teacher wants. He should be trained to answer in order to co-operate with his group and to further the discussion by agreement or disagreement. He should be trained to answer in order to clarify his own thinking. The teacher may not be as clever as some of his pupils, but he should at least be wiser than they are. He plays his part best as guide, counsellor, and friend.

The teacher who indulges in extravagant praise of pupils' answers wastes time and squanders his own proper influence in the classroom. Cold indifference, is, of course, not a characteristic of a good teacher. Judicious praise and honest approval stimulate interest and encourage effort, but the silent commendation of the pupil's classmates is perhaps the most effective reward the pupil can receive for an excellent contribution to the solution of a difficult problem. Only when an answer is obviously insincere or insolently smart should the pupil be reproved; and then only in such a way that his zeal will be turned into more useful channels. It is the teacher's responsibility to find the good that may be present in a sincere answer and to help the pupil to build upon it. So far as possible the pupil's sense of achievement should remain unimpaired.

If, however, pupils are permitted to give superficial answers in a slipshod manner they are being trained in loose and confused habits of thinking and conduct; and thus one of the chief reasons for their presence in school is defeated. Pupils should not be encouraged to answer before thinking out the full purpose of the question, to content themselves with partial or incomplete answers, and to depend on the teacher to stimulate and sustain their effort. Self-reliance is a virtue, and a readiness to accept responsibility for systematic and coherent thinking indicates a consciousness of obligations as well as privileges. Frequently it is possible for a teacher to draw a pupil into an answer that involves careful and sustained thinking, feeling, and imagining. This is an excellent discipline for the whole class if the teacher insists on audibility and correct form, logic, grammar, and use of words. This kind of answer is perhaps the best type of oral composition; it is spontaneous, informal, and completely natural—an opportunity to develop the art of expression. Some questions, of course, require no more than single word answers and it is mere pedantry to require that they be given in the form of complete statements.

The whole class should be given time to think out the answers to questions, but it shows poor judgment to delay a class unreasonably in order to extract answers from a slow pupil. The teacher is expected to incorporate the whole class, but he should not assign a difficult question to a slow pupil, and then proceed to confound him with further questioning. The slow pupil often learns more from listening to the answers of his classmates than from trying to meet the teacher's concerted attack.

If a pupil gives a wrong answer, ask him why he thinks he is right. If he asks you a question, reply by asking him a question that will reveal to him his difficulty, and help him to solve his own problem. If this fails, the question should be thrown open to the class. When a variety of opinions is offered by a number of pupils in answer to a given question, the teacher should clear all points at variance before proceeding with the lesson. It is one thing to stimulate discussion; it is another to guide and control it.

When an answer lacks substance, it may be that the question gave the pupil little provocation to think. Good answers depend somewhat on good questions, and good questions depend somewhat on good preparation. If the teacher is more preoccupied with what is issuing from his own head than with what is entering the heads of his pupils, he is only partially prepared to teach his subject. Before attempting to teach it, he should have asked himself such important questions as the following: What is the purpose of this lesson? What are the pupils to learn from it? What experiences should they apprehend? How may these objectives be best attained? If the teacher sees the needs of his class, he will soon discover his own. Then he will begin to teach with the conviction of experience, and his voice, manner, and attitude will reflect his zeal, leadership, and resourcefulness. This is one way to forestall the common criticism that the teacher belaboured the subject, tried to teach too much, or over-taught some points. In order to teach one fact well, a teacher needs to know a great many. One merit of his lesson will be revealed in the amount of insight, perspective, proportion, emphasis, and restraint he is able to command. He fails hopelessly if he tries to teach to a noisy class or persists in teaching after he has assigned work to be done. Put a restless class to work and let it work! Interruptions of pupils' oral or written responses should be made with great discretion. The less a teacher interferes with the concentration of attention, the less nervous tension he creates in his pupils. Much of the cause for disciplining a class or a pupil originates in the speech or behaviour of the teacher, and there is little excuse for such mistakes in the teaching of subjects that are as interesting as English literature and composition and that afford so many opportunities for mental activity and the development of sound habits of study.

Chapter Six

HE FELL AMONG THIEVES

In the gospel according to St. Luke, Chapter X, is related the parable of the good Samaritan, verses 25-37. Verse 30 reads as follows:

> And Jesus answering said, A certain man went down from Jerusalem to Jericho, and he fell among thieves, which stripped him of his raiment, and wounded him, and departed leaving him half dead.

This passage relates the story of a man who fell among thieves while travelling on one of the best known highways of Biblical times. On it he would hardly expect to fall among thieves, but if perchance he did, he would expect other travellers to come at once to his aid.

From verse 30 Newbolt, a modern English poet, took a statement which he used as the title of a poem, *He Fell Among Thieves*.

T. (Reads the poem aloud.)

'Ye have robb'd,' said he, 'ye have slaughter'd and made an end,
    Take your ill-got plunder, and bury the dead:
What will ye more of your guest and sometime friend?'
    'Blood for our blood,' they said.

He laugh'd: 'If one may settle the score for five,
    I am ready; but let the reckoning stand till day:
I have loved the sunlight as dearly as any alive.'
    'You shall die at dawn,' said they.

He flung his empty revolver down the slope,
    He climb'd alone to the Eastward edge of the trees;
All night long in a dream untroubled of hope
    He brooded, clasping his knees.

He did not hear the monotonous roar that fills
  The ravine where the Yassîn river sullenly flows;
He did not see the starlight on the Laspur hills,
  Or the far Afghan snows.

He saw the April noon on his books aglow,
  The wistaria trailing in at the window wide;
He heard his father's voice from the terrace below
  Calling him down to ride.

He saw the grey little church across the park,
  The mounds that hide the loved and honour'd dead;
The Norman arch, the chancel softly dark,
  The brasses black and red.

He saw the School Close, sunny and green,
  The runner beside him, the stand by the parapet wall,
The distant tape, and the crowd roaring between,
  His own name over all.

He saw the dark wainscot and timber'd roof,
  The long tables, and the faces merry and keen;
The College Eight and their trainer dining aloof,
  The dons on the daïs serene.

He watch'd the liner's stem ploughing the foam,
  He felt her trembling speed and the thrash of her screw;
He heard the passengers' voices talking of home,
  He saw the flag she flew.

And now it was dawn. He rose strong on his feet,
  And strode to his ruin'd camp below the wood;
He drank the breath of the morning cool and sweet:
  His murderers round him stood.

Light on the Laspur hills was broadening fast,
  The blood-red snow-peaks chill'd to a dazzling white;
He turn'd, and saw the golden circle at last,
  Cut by the Eastern height.

'O glorious Life, Who dwellest in earth and sun,
  I have lived, I praise and adore Thee.' A sword swept.
Over the pass the voices one by one
  Faded, and the hill slept.[1]

  [1] Sir Henry Newbolt, *Poems New and Old*. By permission of
the publishers, John Murray, and Captain Francis Newbolt.

T. To what extent is the title of this poem appropriate to its content?

P. The poem tells the story of a man who was robbed, whose companions were slaughtered, and who after a short respite was himself killed. He had thought himself to be among friends.

T.

'Ye have robbed,' said he, 'ye have slaughtered and made an end,
　　Take your ill-got plunder, and bury the dead:
What will ye more of your guest and sometime friend?'
　　'Blood for our blood,' they said.

T. How does the poet try to make this abrupt introduction to his story dramatic—to ring with truth and reality?

P. By giving the actual speech of the characters.

P. The rhythm is strong and rugged, but not rough. The rhyme scheme is simple, but firm.

T. It may interest you to know that this incident is based upon an actual occurrence. About 60 years ago, (probably during the Afghan wars, the last of which began about 1878) Lieutenant Hayward was sent into Afghanistan on an official errand. With his servants he was royally entertained by the Afghans; but the Afghans are a deceitful and treacherous people. When Hayward had completed his mission and planned to leave, the Afghans escorted him and his party to the border, where they made a treacherous attack. This poem tells the remainder of the story as Newbolt saw it in his imagination.

T. Where is the first hint of treachery in this first stanza?

P. "Your guest and sometime friend".

P. "Ill-got plunder".

T.

He laughed: 'If one may settle the score for five,
  I am ready; but let the reckoning stand till day:
I have loved the sunlight as dearly as any alive.'
  'You shall die at dawn,' said they.

T. It is odd that under these circumstances a man should *laugh*. What appeared to be so amusing or ridiculous?

P. Their sense of values may have amused him. They had made the attack, and now show that they were not ready to accept the consequences without revenge.

T. (Note also the typical British attitude—it was a good game while it lasted. All is fair in war, but the British, as a rule, do not kill prisoners. The Afghans had made the attack, but had no sense of sportsmanship. This young officer was game to the last.)

T. What last request did he make of them?

P. That he might live till day-break.

T. Why?

P. That he might see the *sunlight*.

T. Apparently the sun had been to this young man the giver of all good gifts.

T.

He flung his empty revolver down the slope,
  He climbed alone to the Eastward edge of the trees;
All night long in a dream untroubled of hope
  He brooded, clasping his knees.

T. Why did he fling his empty revolver away? (After the class has offered two or three random guesses, they should be referred to the stanza again, and asked to read it silently and carefully for the answer which the poet has given very clearly. Then the pupils will see that with this gesture of finality he flung the revolver away so that he could turn his attention to other things.)

P. Resigned to his fate, he wished to spend his last few hours on earth communing with himself untroubled by any thought of escape or hope for deliverance.

T. By what phrase in this stanza does Newbolt bring vividly before us a typical gesture of an English schoolboy?

P. "Clasping his knees".

T. We see in imagination a boy sitting on a bank at the side of the campus watching a game or waiting his own turn at play. Or we see a boy in the woods beneath a tree or on a hill side, enjoying the English landscape far-flung before him. Finally we see him in this foreign land with the hours of life swiftly ebbing away.

T.

He did not hear the monotonous roar that fills
    The ravine where the Yassîn River sullenly flows;
He did not see the starlight on the Laspur hills,
    Or the far Afghan snows.

He saw the April noon on his books aglow,
    The wistaria trailing in at the window wide;
He heard his father's voice from the terrace below
    Calling him down to ride.

T. In how many ways are these two stanzas in contrast?

P. Details recalled from boyhood days are set off against details of his present surroundings.

P. The *glow* of the April sunlight falling in his dream-picture is in contrast to the starlit darkness that surrounds him. (*Teacher comments on the pronunciation of April.*)

P. The trailing wistaria, so close and friendly in his memory, is in contrast to the far Afghan snows, cold and distant, in this hostile country.

P. The cheery friendly call of his father is in contrast to the dull, heavy, forboding, monotonous roar and the sullen flow of the Yassîn river.

T.

He saw the April noon on his books aglow,
The wistaria trailing in at the window wide;
He heard his father's voice from the terrace below
Calling him down to ride.

T. As young Hayward recollects his early boyhood days in this first picture that rises to his mind, two experiences stand out. What are they?

P. His interest in books and companionship.

T. In the light of his later career in general and the manner of his death in particular, with what subject may we suppose these books to have dealt?

P. Adventure.

T. What may he have learned from his companionship with his father?

P. He may have learned what it is to be a man and a sportsman.

T.

He saw the gray little church across the park,
The mounds that hide the loved and honour'd dead;
The Norman arch, the chancel softly dark,
The brasses black and red.

T. What are the details of the second picture that rises in his reverie?

P. The gray little church with the Norman arch, the mounds of the dead and the chancel and brasses.

T. In the previous stanza there is a line that shows his sensitiveness in the presence of beautiful objects with pleasant associations, "The wistaria trailing in at the window wide". What words in this stanza show the same sensitiveness and perception?

P. "Gray little church", "Norman arch", "softly dark", "black and red".

T. Why did the *mounds* interest him?

P. They were the last resting place of the honoured dead.

T. Why were they honoured?

P. For the services they had in life performed for their fellow men—their country.

T. Why are these brasses or plaques placed on the inner walls of churches?

P. They are memorials erected in honour of persons from the community who had performed great services to their country in the form of great thoughts or great deeds.

T. If these details recur so vividly to him now, they must have made a great impression on him as a boy. Perhaps they played a part in the shaping of his character and career. What effect did these things, the memorials, the mounds, have on him as a boy?

P. Probably they stirred his ambition to emulate the splendid achievements of these heroes.

T.

He saw the School Close, sunny and green,
   The runner beside him, the stand by the parapet wall,
The distant tape, and the crowd roaring between
   His own name over all.

T. What are the details of this picture?

P. The playground bright with sunlight and eager faces. The excitement of the crowd and his own enthusiasm as they cheer him to a winning finish.

T.

He saw the dark wainscot and timber'd roof,
    The long tables, and the faces merry and keen,
The College Eight and their trainer dining aloof,
    The Dons on the daïs serene.

T. Where is he now?

P. He has gone up from school to college.

T. What details show that life at college was to him a pleasant recollection?

P. The very timbers of the place, "dark wainscot and timbered roof", had endeared themselves to him. He sees in reverie the old dining-hall, the undergraduate tables, and on a platform or daïs at the end of the hall the "training-table" and the "faculty-table".

(NOTE—*dais* may be pronounced dace or daïs but never dias. Here the rhythm demands daïs.)

T. In the first picture (stanza 5) and the third picture (stanza 7) one discovers that this boy took a keen interest in sport and athletic achievement. At which table would he probably see himself seated in the fourth picture (this stanza 8)?

P. At the training-table as a member of the winning rowing crew.

T. What difference can you discover between this athletic experience and the previous one?

P. In the third picture (previous stanza) he recalls the day he made a name for himself. In this stanza (the fourth picture) he recalls the day he won honour for his college by co-operating with his fellows.

T. Why is this an important step in the boy's development?

P. He felt the thrill of team-work.

T.

He watch'd the liner's stem ploughing the foam,
  He felt her trembling speed and the thrash of her screw;
He heard the passengers' voices talking of home,
  He saw the flag she flew.

T. Which way is the vessel going, to or from England? (After a very brief debate the class will be led to see that the vessel is going out from England because it is more customary for people to talk of home outward bound than when inward bound. Still a better reason for this belief is found in the fact that this stanza presents the fifth and last picture from the young man's "dream untroubled of hope". As a climax to the series, home, church, school, college, this stanza shows him entering upon his life's work in service for his country with his eye steadily fixed upon the British flag and all that it represents. "He saw the flag she flew.")

T. "And now it was dawn." What has the poet gained by breaking this line in the middle?

P. It brings his dream to an abrupt end. It makes vivid the contrast between his reverie and reality by breaking suddenly and completely the rhythm of the thought.

T. "He rose strong on his feet." Whence came this strength?

P. It came from his recollections of his past. His dream afforded him a refreshing respite. This final act of giving his life in the service of his country was the climax to a career that had apparently been dedicated to his country. He rose strong to face the test.

T. "And strode to his ruined camp below the wood."
What word in this line sustains our opinion of this man?

P. "Strode".

T. Why is it a better word here than *walked*?

P. It brings before us the figure of a man of strong
courage going resolutely and deliberately to meet his fate.

T. "He drank the breath of the morning cool and
sweet." Why is this more appropriate and poetic than to
say, "He breathed the air of the morning cool and sweet"?

P. He drank it as the wine of life—the elixir.

T. Justify the sentence the poet passes on Hayward's
captors in the line, "His murderers round him stood."

P. Once the bloody skirmish was at an end, the Afghans had no other reason than that of murder for killing
this innocent captive who had merely fought for his life.

T.

Light on the Laspur hills was broadening fast,
  The blood-red snow-peaks chilled to a dazzling white;
He turned, and saw the golden circle at last,
  Cut by the Eastern height.

T. Why is the material of this stanza introduced at this
point?

P. It brings the dawn and the sunlight which Hayward
had asked to see.

T. What word brings the rising sun vividly before us?

P. The word *cut.*

T. Not only does this stanza show his wish fulfilled; it
brings the reader back to the setting etched in stanza 4.

T.

'O glorious Life, Who dwellest in earth and sun,
  I have lived, I praise and adore Thee.' A sword swept.
Over the pass the voices one by one
  Faded, and the hill slept.

T. In Hayward's career what may the substance of this brief prayer stand for?

P. His creed.

T. In what words is it stated?

P. "I have lived," and this creed sustains him to the end.

T. To whom is it addressed?

P. To Life.

T. Now let us see in how many ways the short statement "A sword swept", is poetically appropriate.

P. In thought it is appropriate because it states a merciless deed in the briefest and most merciful form.

T. What is its value emotionally?

P. The slaying is over in an instant and the reader's feelings are not harrowed by horrifying details nor his attention fixed upon the bloody deed. Anything more than this would have been melodramatic.

T. What is its auditory value?

P. The sound is short, smooth and sure. The combination of sounds—the two words *sword swept*—suggests a clean finality. It allows no time for the reader to image the deed.

T. What is its rhythmic value?

P.

I have lived, I praise and adore Thee.' A sword swept.

Rhythmically the important words stand alone as a spondaic foot, and this condition increases the other values of these words.

T. Read the last two lines in a hushed voice. How many sounds here fall softly on the ear?

P. Over, one by one, faded, slept.

T. Why are these sounds and statements appropriate here?

P. They bring down the curtain swiftly and silently, and the poem closes in eternal peace.

T. In this poem the poet has given the facts of the story as he has felt them and seen them in his imagination. He has carefully avoided sentimentality, patriotism, and vain-glorying in victory over enemies or death. On what fact then has he tried to fix the attention of the reader?

P. The reader is left with the thought deeply impressed on him that Hayward died bravely and nobly—a credit to the country that bore him—and won undying honour by his sacrifice.

T. Newbolt comes from a family that has distinguished itself by its services to Britain and the Empire. For many generations this patriotic family has produced officers for the British navy. Newbolt the poet was trained in law and in this vocation served his country in peace and war. For his poems he found inspiration in two fountains that are subterraneously joined and rise from the same source. Judging by his poems he was inspired by the deeds of English heroes and by the character of the English school boy. In the light of these facts why do you think he was attracted by the incident that gave rise to this moving poem?

PP. (*A composite answer.*) Evidently he believed that the chain is no stronger than its separate links. The welfare of the British Empire rests in the hands of its individual members. Responsibility for the Empire is a duty incumbent on each one of us. Hayward played his part nobly. The manner of his sacrifice was tangible evidence of his training and set a diamond not a blot upon the escutcheon of the Empire he served, despite the fact that he had fallen into the hands of thieves and murderers.

NOTES AND COMMENTS ON THE TEACHING OF
He Fell Among Thieves

Short narrative poems should be studied as single units of thought and emotion. The poet intended that all parts should be seen in the light of the whole. If the five stanzas of reverie in the middle of this poem are separated from what precedes and follows them, the purpose and effectiveness of the larger unit to which they belong is impaired. The poet did not allot four stanzas to the introduction, five to the body, and three to the conclusion of this poem. The poem is one unit and should be so preserved. The fifth stanza is thrown into relief by the sharp contrast it makes with the fourth, and the tenth stanza serves as a climax to the five stanzas that precede it.

Aim to give appropriate emphasis to salient details rather than exhaustive treatment to every unimportant fact. A whole stanza may be opened up by one question, "Why did he throw the revolver away?" or "Which way was the vessel going?" Time and effort spent on the examination of the mortar-words in a structure and on the probing of facts of less than adjacent interest to the story, will exhaust the patience of a whole class and perhaps turn them from poetry forever. Observe how futile and fatuous are the following questions. Their answers contribute nothing to the central thought and feeling of the story. Why was the revolver empty? What is a terrace? What is a parapet? What did the tape represent? What is a timbered roof? What is a liner's stem? What happened when the sword swept? And the question that reaches a high point in sentimentality: Did this young man study at home in his early boyhood because he was too delicate in health to go to school?

Unable to apprehend a theme in the poem *He Fell Among Thieves,* some teachers dwell upon the botanical history of the wistaria, the history of Norman architecture, the use of flags on merchant ships, the derivation of *liner* as a ship belonging to a series of steamships, the geographical position of the Laspur hills and the Yassîn river. These excursions into botany, architecture, and geography, even when accompanied by illustrative pictures and maps, have nothing whatever to do with the fact that this young Briton acquitted himself bravely in the line of duty to which his ideals led him, and was, when put to the final test, a worthy representative of the land that bred him, but these excursions impress the class with the teacher's industry and erudition. And nothing will take the minds of the pupils off the poem more completely than the passing of pictures of vines and arches around the class. This kind of exhaustive treatment of literature disgusts the better pupils and deludes the poorer ones.

Such belabouring of a poem, for instance, with cloudy talk about non-essentials provides a ready smoke-screen for the teacher's lack of insight. It underestimates the natural ability of the majority of pupils. It is convincing evidence of the teacher's incompetence in handling both subject and method, and when his own weariness is reflected in his class he seeks escape in the "freedom" of extensive reading and claims that his pupils are incapable

of anything else. What they need, he thinks, is more and
more casual and superficial reading of many books.
Intensive study he condemns because he does not know
on what to lay emphasis. He does not understand the
nature of his subject or the purposes for which it is taught.
If the teacher is so woefully lacking in discernment, what
chance is there that his pupils will ever acquire a dis-
criminating taste? With all his clamour for "freedom for
the teacher" and "enjoyment for the pupil", the incompetent teacher merely aims to deliver his pupils into the
hands of unscrupulous propagandists. For all his apparent
anxiety for the pupils of other teachers, he is chiefly
anxious to get away from his own—to lose himself completely in the self-glorification of post-graduate study. If
he is not of much use as a teacher, he can, at least, pretend
to be an educationist.

The purpose of sound education in English literature
is to increase the pupil's power to discover and assimilate
imaginative experience, to lead him to perceive the principles and the significances that underlie the realities of
both life and literature, and to direct his creative energies
to the building of sound character.

Some readers may contend that the interpretation of
this poem has been forced. The reverse of this is more
likely to be true. The aim of the teacher should be to seek
the intention of the poet rather than to reveal his own
sentimentality or prejudice.

A few years ago when a class had completed the study
of *He Fell Among Thieves,* a young man asked with a
sneer, "Do you believe all that?" What he wished to
know, of course, was whether I was in sympathy with the

heroism portrayed in the poem. It was evident that he was not, and, like other intellectuals, he wished to impress others with his superciliousness. My reply to this pacifist was that we must be honest with the poet and read him as we find him, that Newbolt was an Imperialist who laboured all his life for Britain and the Empire, and that my personal or political views had nothing to do with the subject in hand. He was not satisfied, but I found it difficult to speak, remembering the men I knew who died on the Somme and at Passchendaele to make the world safe for such clever careful people as my self-expressive questioner.

Chapter Seven

THE TIGER

T. What is your impression of any tiger you have seen?

P. I saw a tiger once at the Zoo, and it looked like a big sleepy cat.

P. I saw one in a circus once, and it was sly and sneaky. It snarled at its trainer as it jumped like a cat from box to box.

T. Yes, Ralph Hodgson, a modern British poet, describes a tiger in captivity as a "tamed and shabby" creature. What is your impression of any tiger you have read about in story books?

P. Any tigers I have read about were always sleek and fierce and cunning. In the jungle they are hunted from the backs of elephants, and this is described as a very dangerous sport.

T. One traveller summed up his impression of the jungle tiger in the words, "The tiger-haunted night is a reign of terror." Apparently impressions differ with the points from which the beast is regarded. Here is how William Blake, a famous British poet, viewed a tiger:

(Teacher reads aloud.)

Tiger, tiger, burning bright
In the forests of the night,
What immortal hand or eye
Could frame thy fearful symmetry?

In what distant deeps or skies
Burnt the fire of thine eyes?
On what wings dare he aspire?
What the hand dare seize the fire?

148

And what shoulder and what art
Could twist the sinews of thy heart?
And, when thy heart began to beat,
What dread hand and what dread feet?

What the hammer? What the chain?
In what furnace was thy brain?
What the anvil? What dread grasp
Dare its deadly terrors clasp?

When the stars threw down their spears,
And watered heaven with their tears,
Did He smile His work to see?
Did He who made the lamb make thee?

Tiger, tiger, burning bright,
In the forests of the night,
What immortal hand or eye
Dare frame thy fearful symmetry?

What was Blake's impression of the tiger?

P. It was a strong, fierce beast.

P. It was something to be feared.

P. Blake wondered who could make such a fearsome creature as the tiger.

T. Yes. These are all true. His feelings were a mixture of fear and wonder; but where did Blake see his tiger?

P. He said, "In the forests of the night".

P. How could he see it, if it were dark?

P. He could see its eyes shining.

T. Now read the poem silently. Perhaps you can discover where Blake really saw his tiger.

P. Blake saw this tiger in his imagination.

T. How do you know?

P. He imagined he saw the tiger being constructed in a foundry or a blacksmith shop.

T. Yes. The poet does mention tools that a blacksmith uses, but I cannot agree with your opinion that he imagined he saw a tiger being constructed or created. Read the poem again.

P. He saw the tiger in his imagination, and he wondered how it was created.

T. That is better. Blake saw the tiger whole, and then he wondered who could create such a beast. Now, let us see what the tiger looked like that Blake imagined, and why he felt as he did when he saw it isolated in his imagination. Please read the first stanza aloud.

P.

> Tiger, tiger, burning bright
> In the forests of the night,
> What immortal hand or eye
> Could frame thy fearful symmetry?

T. What feature or quality of the tiger attracted Blake's attention first?

P. Its shape.

P. Its colour.

P. Its strength.

T. Perhaps; but Blake did not say so. You will have to use your imaginations if you are to see what Blake saw. Read the stanza carefully again.

P. He saw the piercing light in the tiger's eyes, blazing out of the dark background of "the forests of the night".

T. Piercing and *blazing* are apt words. How did the poet suggest them to you?

P. He saw the fire in the tiger's eyes "burning", not merely shining or glowing; "bright" suggests something sharper and more piercing than "brightly" would.

T. That is good. What did Blake imagine lay behind this fire "burning bright"?

P. He saw the sleek and powerful and wonderfully proportioned body of the tiger.

T. Where did you find these ideas?

P. He said it had symmetry. Its body was magnificently proportioned. It was this smooth, harmonious form, so perfectly balanced in all its parts, that fascinated the poet. He wondered who "could frame" it.

T. He may have been fascinated by its form, but what particular feeling did its symmetry arouse in him?

P. He was "fearful" of it.

P. He wondered who could make such a creature.

T. Whoever did, employed both "hand" and "eye". How would you distinguish between their uses in this connection?

P. By the eye he would be able to see the shape he wished to make, and by the hand he would be able to construct it.

T. Who would?

P. He did not say.

T. I think he did.

P. Oh, yes! Whoever did, must be immortal.

T. And what may we infer from that?

P. A mortal could not create the tiger. Only God could frame its symmetry and put within the creature such strange fire as burns in the tiger's eyes.

T. That is true, but it does not express all the meaning that Blake implied. Try again.

P. Only God would have the insight to conceive the design, and only God would have the skill and power to construct it.

T. Excellent.   Several times you have said that Blake was *wondering*. Where did you get that idea?

P. For one thing, he is not stating facts; he is asking questions. The whole poem is a series of questions.

T. To whom are these questions addressed?

P. To the tiger.

T. To what particular tiger?

P. The one he saw in his imagination.

T. Since the poet knew that God alone could answer his questions, what may be the significance of addressing them to the tiger?

P. He may have seen God's hand and purpose behind it all.

P. Perhaps he saw God in the tiger.

T. And what may he have seen shining through the fierce light in the tiger's eyes?

P. The power of God.

T. To whom, then, was the poet indirectly paying tribute?

P. To God.

T. What feelings were aroused in Blake as this fire, animal or divine, pierced his imagination?

P. He wondered where it came from, and he stood in fear and awe of it. He was probably thinking of the Creator of the tiger.

T. Now read the stanza again. Read it aloud quickly without giving attention to the meaning. Of what familiar verse does it remind you?

P.

> Twinkle, twinkle, little star,
>   How I wonder what you are,
> Up above the world so high,
>   Like a diamond in the sky.

T. Why is this same form and rhythm appropriate to Blake's theme?

P. They are well suited to Blake's child-like attitude of questioning and wondering as he stood before the "unexplainable".

T. Confronted by the inexplicable he felt awe and perhaps terror, and this was reflected even in the form and rhythm of the poem. How is this feeling intensified in the next stanza? Read it aloud, please.

P.

> In what distant deeps or skies
> Burnt the fire of thine eyes?
> On what wings dare he aspire?
> What the hand dare seize the fire?

The questions come quickly and more insistently.

P. Blake wondered where this strange "fire" in the tiger's eyes came from, who *could* soar to the distant heavens—perhaps to the stars or the sun—to procure it, but most of all, who would "dare" to do so and to take this fire in his hands.

T. To what, then, was he still paying tribute?

P. To the mysterious power of God.

T. Read the next two stanzas, please.

P.

> And what shoulder and what art
> Could twist the sinews of thy heart?
> And, when thy heart began to beat,
> What dread hand and what dread feet?

> What the hammer?   What the chain?
> In what furnace was thy brain?
> What the anvil?   What dread grasp
> Dare its deadly terrors clasp?

T. Again the questions come thick and fast, even jerkily, as images tumble into the poet's mind. Where did Blake imagine he saw God at work?

P. He saw God as a mighty blacksmith, with hammer and anvil, working at his forge and moulding the tiger.

T. And what feature was He moulding (stanza 3)?

P. Its heart?

T. How did he do it?

P. With the superhuman strength of a huge shoulder and the skill and imagination of a supreme artist, God "twists" the sinews of the tiger's heart to the shape and temper that His divine mind desires.

T. Yes. Both hand and eye, both physical and mental strength, are involved in the creation of this symbol of infinite perfection. And as Blake watched, he imagined he heard the great heart beating. Can you hear it throbbing through the rhythm?

P.

$$\cup \quad / \quad \cup \quad / \quad \cup / \quad \cup \quad /$$
And when | thy heart | began | to beat |
$$/ \quad - \quad / \quad \cup \quad / \quad - \quad /$$
What | dread hand | and what | dread feet? |

T. The meaning of the last line of this stanza may seem a little obscure. In the first draft of the poem Blake continued as follows:

stanza 3.   What dread hand and what dread feet

stanza 4.   Could filch it from the furnace deep
And in thy hornèd ribs dare steep
In the well of sanguine woe
(incomplete)

What interpretation of the line can we infer from this?

P. In the last line of stanza 3, Blake was still thinking of the superhuman power of God.

T. Yes. Although poets and editors, anxious to make the question grammatically sound, have pedantically substituted *formed* or *forged* for "and" in this line, the line, corrupt but clipped in both sense and sound as Blake left it, best expresses the stark awe Blake felt as he envisioned the endowments of the tiger's creator. In *The Hound of Heaven* Francis Thompson used a similar image, "From those strong feet that followed, followed after." What word intensifies this feeling in Blake's line?

P. The emotional word "dread" is repeated.

T. It is repeated again in the next stanza. In what connection is it used there? Before answering, make sure of the antecedent of "its" in the last line.

P. Blake felt a strange cold fear as he imagined the mighty effort of the Creator who would "dare" to grasp the "deadly terrors" that went into the making of the tiger's brain.

T. How does the rhythm of line 3 support this interpretation?

P.

$$\text{/} \quad \smile \quad \text{/} \quad \smile \quad \text{/} \quad - \quad \text{/}$$

What | the an | vil?   What | dread grasp |

The line moves slowly and heavily with the effort involved.

T. If Blake ascribed to the tiger's heart and brain such primitive force and deadly terrors, with what must he have endowed the tiger's creator?

P. With vision and inventive ingenuity far beyond man's capacity to comprehend.

T. Blake's theme is profound, but so far his expression has been extremely simple, and his meaning almost crystal clear. How did he make us see so clearly what he saw?

P. His images are all commonplace, definite, and concrete, like *shoulder, sinews, hand, feet, hammer, anvil,* etc.

P. He seemed to be under a spell or in a trance, and everything appeared clearly etched in his imagination.

T. Blake was an engraver, and this fact may have had something to do with the way in which his meaning and imagery are interwoven.

In the next stanza the meaning is almost lost in the imagery.

> When the stars threw down their spears,
> And watered heaven with their tears,
> Did He smile His work to see?
> Did He who made the lamb make thee?

What apparently happened in heaven when God created the tiger?

P.

> the stars threw down their spears,
> And watered heaven with their tears.

T. These lines have received several interpretations. What is yours?

P. This may be a beautiful picture of the starry heavens at the time of creation.

P. The stars may have wept in fear at the sight of the fierce, destructive tiger.

P. Perhaps the hosts of heaven wept because they did not and could not understand God's purposes.

T. These are all interesting. Here are other ways in which these lines have been interpreted:

"The stars become symbols of peace and love. Weeping, they question speechlessly the meaning of the presence of such pitiless cruelty."

"The whole universe bows before the God who has done this thing. Even the stars are sorrowful with fear at what such a creature may do."

It has even been suggested that when order out of chaos became apparent in the universe "the fighting stars became repentant and gave up the strife." It would be like Blake to think so.

But more important than these two lines is the question Blake put again to the tiger:

> Did He smile His work to see?

Originally Blake wrote "laugh", but in revising he changed "laugh" to "smile". Which is more consistent with the meaning of the poem as we have interpreted it?

P. "Laugh" suggests that the Creator was amused at what he had done; "smile" suggests a satisfaction, not indulgent but impenetrable.

T. It is what might be called an inscrutable smile, the meaning of which cannot be understood. Why, then, is "smile" more appropriate?

P. God's purposes are hidden from men.

T. What contrast is contained in the last question of this stanza?

P. The tiger is contrasted with the lamb, power with gentleness.

T. And, perhaps, even experience with innocence. But what is the significance of this question?

P. Blake was now wondering not only *how* but also *why* the tiger was created.

T. The poet returned in the last stanza to his original question, and rounded off his poem by a repetition with one slight but significant change. What change did he make?

P. He asked now who would *dare* to create the tiger.

T. Who holds the answer to that question?

P. God.

T. That is what the poet discovered. In an earlier poem, *The Lamb,* published before the French Revolution, in his collection called *The Songs of Innocence,* Blake began:

> Little lamb who made thee?
> Dost thou know who made thee?

and in the first of two stanzas asked a series of questions like these, but in the second stanza he answered them. In *The Tiger,* published after the French Revolution, in his collection entitled *Songs of Experience,* Blake, as we have discovered, left his questions unanswered. Wicksteed, Blake's best interpreter, comments thus: "If God is manifest as the Lamb 'by the stream and o'er the mead', He can reveal Himself equally 'in the forests of the night' as the Tiger. And when night yields to day it is a greater day." But Blake was now content to raise questions, to see by faith the majesty and might of the Lord and marvel at His power. He was too wise to seek an answer by any form of human reasoning. One of his contemporaries,

however, thought he could. William Paley (1743-1805) in
his book *Evidences of Christianity* tried, for instance, to
establish the possibility of miracles by logic alone. He
based his arguments for religion on a kind of utilitar-
ianism, on reason rather than revelation. How would
Blake's poem fit into this rationalistic scheme?

P. It would not fit in at all.

T. Why not?

P. Throughout the poem Blake assumes the presence
of a living God, an "immortal hand or eye", whose plans
and purposes he could not understand, but whose infinite
wisdom and genius inspired him with awe and wonder.

T. What, then, might we say of Blake's "beliefs" when
he wrote *The Tiger*?

P. Blake must have been a man of great spiritual faith.

T. Yes. This was Blake's vision as the fierce starry
light in the tiger's eyes blazed through his imagination.
Now read the whole poem aloud to express what Blake
saw and thought and felt.

*PP. (Two or three pupils—preferably volunteers—read
in turn the whole poem.)*

T. After reading this poem for the first time Charles
Lamb declared the author to be "one of the most extraordinary persons of the age". How can you justify this
statement by reference to the poem?

P. For one thing Blake succeeded in putting a great
deal in a very small space.

T. Explain.

PP. (A composite answer.) The theme is profound
enough. The relationship of man to God is a deep subject
for a lyric so brief as this is. And it is well done—not too

much and not too little—a finished piece. Every line of it seems to be alive with a spontaneous energy. Moreover it is all in question form, and that makes it more original and challenging. The language is unusually simple. The images we can see very clearly; we seem able to get a mental grip on them—perhaps because Blake saw them first with extraordinary intensity, with the eye of an engraver or an artist.

T. That is all true. What else do you suppose would appeal to Charles Lamb?

PP. (A composite answer.) The way in which Blake took the tiger and gradually made it a symbol of terror is evidence of great poetic power. Before the poem is finished, we realize that Blake is not so much interested in the tiger as a wild beast as he is in all the invisible or intangible things that the tiger's form, power, and animal spirit suggest to his imagination.

P. Perhaps Lamb was interested in Blake's simple childlike questioning, and his deep personal faith.

T. Perhaps, too, Lamb saw in this poem the counterpart of an imaginative experience that was new, fresh, direct, and immediate in its appeal—an earnestness and sincerity that were forthright. Among the worn reeds of the weary classicists Lamb may have seen in Blake's hands a new instrument capable of expressing an individual lyric intensity that had not been heard in England for many a long year. Blake was not merely a forerunner of the "romanticists", but like Burns in Scotland, he was an independent and audacious pioneer who set the pace for other men to follow. He subscribed to no rules, but those dictated by his own will.

But still more likely, Lamb saw behind this poem a man who had something really significant to say, a man who by the intensity of his imaginative fire had blazed a course clear through the commonplace platitudes and facile banalities of other men to find beyond their tangled undergrowth a pleasant valley strangely wonderful, where spiritual peace and happiness abound. Lamb, doubtless, saw in Blake a seer of visions and a dreamer of dreams, truly "one of the most extraordinary persons of the age".

In Blake's *The Tiger* you have seen the divine blacksmith in action. If you will turn to Francis Thompson's *To a Snowflake* you will see the divine jeweller at work.

What heart would have thought you?—
Past our devisal
(O filagree petal!)
Fashioned so purely,
Fragilely, surely,
From what Paradisal
Imagineless metal,
Too costly for cost?
Who hammered you, wrought you,
From argentine vapour?—
"God was my shaper
Passing surmisal,
He hammered, He wrought me,
From curled silver vapour,
To lust of His mind:—
Thou couldst not have thought me!
So purely, so palely,
Tinily, surely,
Mightily, frailly,
Insculped and embossed,
With His hammer of wind,
And His graver of frost.[1]

[1] Francis Thompson, *To a Snowflake*. By permission of the publishers, Burns, Oates & Washbourne Ltd.

T. What has this poem in common with *The Tiger?*

P. The moods of both poems are much the same.

P. Both deal with the same theme—the mystery of God's creative power.

P. In both we see God at work with the tools of his trade, creating things wonderful to behold.

P. In one questions are addressed to a tiger; in the other questions are addressed to a snowflake. The snowflake, however, replies; the tiger does not.

T. What other differences do you notice?

P. The images and words used in *To a Snowflake* are more delicately fanciful and descriptive than those used in *The Tiger.*

P. The rhyme scheme is more complicated or intricate: *a b b c c b b d a e e b c e f c c c c d f d*; and the rhyming sounds *ou, al, me, ost, er, ind,* are sharply contrasted with one another.

P. The rhythm too is different:

$$\smile \quad / \quad \smile \quad \smile \quad / \quad \smile$$

What heart would | have thought you

The predominating rhythm throughout the poem is amphibrachic dimetre with here and there a substituted trochee, iambus, or anapest for greater variety.

T. What do all these elements contribute to the theme? You have mentioned the delicate imagery, the fanciful language, the intricate rhyme scheme, the lilting rhythm.

P. They all help by statement or suggestion to describe a snowflake—its fragility and crystal-like perfection of form.

T. What does *The Tiger* gain by this comparison?

P. We see the greater simplicity, intensity, and profundity of Blake's vision and faith.

T. Excellent! If you have found inspiration in *The Tiger*, you will wish to borrow this collection of Blake's poems chosen from his *Songs of Innocence* and his *Songs of Experience*. Any of them will well repay your careful reading; some will challenge all your power to think, to feel, to see. Try either of these stanzas, for instance:

> To see a World in a grain of sand
> And a Heaven in a wild flower,
> Hold Infinity in the palm of your hand
> And Eternity in an hour.

or this:

> I will not cease from Mental Fight
> Nor shall my Sword sleep in my hand,
> Till we have built Jerusalem
> In England's green and pleasant land.

NOTES AND COMMENTS ON TEACHING *The Tiger*

Questions should always be as concise and direct as it is possible to make them; and easy questions should precede difficult ones. As the lesson proceeds, the pupils gain confidence in interpreting, and their answers consequently improve in content and expression. In order to save space, two or more spoken answers are sometimes combined into one written answer. The sequence of images, thoughts, and feelings is traceable through the questions and answers, but nothing is regarded as merely mechanical, no matter how splendidly logical may appear to be the organization of the material of the poem.

The tiger is used metaphorically, but this fact is of far less importance than the realization that the tiger actually confronts us in imagination and may inspire feelings of awe and wonder. Blake doubtless had in mind both the Old and the New Testaments. Unless the pupil recognizes the power of God behind the "immortal hand" referred to in the first stanza, his imagination is not even turned in the direction of the poet's vision. Care must be taken, however, not to emphasize one image or thought at the expense of the whole; there is no need to preach a sermon on "Did He who made the lamb make thee?"

The teacher's aim should be to go directly, quickly, and firmly to the heart of experience, to use the exposition of the poet's theme and the revelation of an artistic masterpiece as aids to the pupils in the creation for themselves of similar imaginative and aesthetic experiences.

"Twinkle, twinkle, little star" is introduced here to simplify a point; it has no other connection with Blake's poem, since it was written by Jane Taylor in 1804.

Pupils soon accustom themselves to the teacher's way of looking at things, his manner of speech, and his phrasing of ideas. Let the teacher, then, set a high standard, and the pupils will reach upward and grow by stretching. Young teachers, who feel that in order to teach high school pupils they must come down to what they call "the pupil's level", are already below it, and are facing in the wrong direction to see their pupils' needs and their own opportunities.

If the teacher of English will remember that not the least of his duties in the classroom is the cultivation of sound habits of literary study, he will take advantage of every opportunity to lay stress upon the significance of language and the observation and interpretation of details and structures in literary art as bases of appreciation of literature and as foundations for exactness and clarity of thought and expression.

Properly taught, a boy who can learn how a machine is constructed and operated, or a girl who can design and make a dress, can also learn how to apprehend literary experience and to appreciate standards of value in the literary art. The same faculties and qualities are brought into play in all these activities, namely observation, analysis, classification, interpretation, integration, synthesis, and composition. The chief difference lies in the fact that the one operation takes place before the eye and the other in the mind's eye; but the important fact is that experience in either one of these activities enhances and makes for greater competence and success in the other.

From some teachers of English one hears too much defeatism—"The pupils are not interested. . . They have not enough vocabulary to express their ideas. . . They do not like English. . . They have to be entertained. . . They do not want to think. . . They do not know how to read. . . They do not take the work seriously." Here is the teacher's opportunity, but he must first rid himself of literary affectation and sophistication, and set to work to teach literature. English is English no matter in what type of school it is taught.

Chapter Eight

THE TEACHER OF ENGLISH

In the light of the foregoing theory and practice, the character of the teacher becomes highly significant. The degree of the teacher's success in winning the surrender of his pupils to the subject and in inspiring them to the apprehension of imaginative experience will depend, to some extent, on the kind of person that the teacher is. No matter how objective he tries to be, his beliefs and attitudes are bound to become entangled with the material that he teaches. Not everyone who is twenty-one years of age and who speaks the English language is a fit and proper person to teach English literature. Regardless even of academic qualifications, some people are better suited than others to the task, and within the more competent group there is space enough for variety. The thing most desired in the teaching of English today is an intensive and systematic method of study. If, then, a few comments, based on some years of observation, are recited here, the young teacher of English will not, it is hoped, be so self-conscious as to feel that he is being rendered into a type. It may be, however, that he will take up the challenge of some statements and interpret them in his own personal way for better or for worse. This, at least, is the spirit in which these comments are offered.

Among the greatest assets of the teacher of English are a generous portion of common sense, a sense of humour, a sense of perspective, a sense of proportion, and a sense of wonder. In short it would appear that he must be a person of considerable sensibility, but not in the sense in which the psychologist would define the term or the sentimentalist apply it. Without a sense of wonder, the teacher's sense of perspective may remain mundane. Without a sense of humour, his sense of proportion may become distorted. Humour is the safety-valve of the mind; it preserves the equilibrium of common sense, keeps the mind open to wonder, and enlarges its capacity for clear perspective. In the classroom, wit may "save the day", but a sense of humour saves the very life of the teacher. Unless he can laugh at himself, he is a person of less than common sense.

In his handling of his subject the teacher of English needs insight, imagination, and industry. Insight without industry affords a spectacle almost as pitiable as industry without insight. But it is not enough that the teacher be a person of industry and insight; he must be able to inspire insight and industry in others. If he would interest others in what he is interested in, it follows that he should be a person who is himself easily bored. His task, like all other high endeavours, requires a fertile imagination. From his powers of speculation and reflection often spring his insight, the readiness of his adaptability, the quality of his resourcefulness, and his ability to raise thought-provoking questions and to guide discussion to worthy ends. And these qualities, by the way, are a few of the attributes of leadership.

The chancellor of a university has no power to confer leadership. This fact seems difficult for young teachers to understand. Leadership is an endowment placed on the teacher partly by those whom he teaches. He may command their obedience, but not their respect. Now from this it should not be construed that the teacher must try to "win friends and influence people" or seek the temporary satisfaction of cheap popularity.

> All men my brothers? I must love all these?
> 'Twill take some doing: but what must, must be . . .
> Though, God preserve me, if, in their turn, they
> Should all start loving me![1]

The power to inculcate loyalties springs from a deeper source than á sadist's desire to subjugate another's will. Genuine leadership is a gift made in recognition of personal worth. Once received, however, it should be translated into action; if it is held merely as a trust, it ceases to be leadership. What a teacher knows and what he can do are important; what he *is,* however, is paramount. He may be a person of broad scholarship and great technical skill, but unless there is behind his action some integrity and stability of character, his pupils may echo Emerson and ask "How can I hear what you say when what you are keeps thundering in my ears?"

Among the greatest teachers have been those who were not afraid to look into their deeper selves, who could find there an inner peace—a serenity of spirit, and who were able to speak with the conviction of experience. "It is a definite religious belief which gives a man the highest conception of his work as a schoolmaster." Without such belief, the terms co-operation and goodwill are likely

[1] Wilfrid Gibson, *In Piccadilly Circus* from *Coming and Going.* Oxford.

to be relative to circumstances and expediency. No matter how interesting are the facts of the lesson or how efficient is the skill with which they are presented, the purpose of the lesson is impaired unless the teacher understands the meaning behind the facts and appreciates the value of the ends towards which they are so earnestly marshalled. The teacher who thinks that the purpose of education is only to impart information to those who have the strength or the wit to reach for it knows very little about his job. "For we walk by faith, not by sight".[1] And faith takes courage—the courage to face the fact of "One's own self"—to live at close quarters with one's self.

> Far safer, of a midnight, meeting
> External ghost,
> Than an interior confronting,
> That whiter host.
>
> Far safer through an Abbey gallop,
> The stones achase,
> Than, moonless, one's own self encounter
> In lonesome place.[2]

Among the greatest teachers of English have been those who could find a living interest in their subjects for their pupils, because they had more than a perfunctory interest in their work and in children. They had high ideals, generous instincts, intelligent sympathy, and abiding zeal; but they had none of that spurious

---

[1] *Corinthians* II, 5:7.

[2] Emily Dickinson, *One need not be a chamber to be haunted* from *The Poems of Emily Dickinson*, edited by Martha Dickinson Bianchi and Alfred Lute Hampson. Reprinted by permission of Little, Brown & Company.

enthusiasm of men who believe in a self-appointed mission. They escaped the restlessness of those confined to a state of arrested development. Impatient with stifling intellectualism, exhausting emotionalism, and restricting aestheticism, they avoided the pitfalls of pedantry, pomposity, and cynicism, and were able consequently to keep their balance. Self-realization, not self-satisfaction, was their aim for their pupils. Their hope was to be able to do a plain job well. They did not pretend to be bigger or better than they were, but tried to be themselves at their best all the time. They were builders of characters, not social reconstructionists. They suffered from no "uplift" complex, because they felt none of that arrogant superiority that sets off the intellectuals from the rest of mankind. Their pupils were not given the impression that they were being taught for their intellectual improvement or cultural advancement. Their feelings were not whipped to a froth of excitement and doomed to disappointment. They were *taught* and *trained* by men who feared God, honoured the king, and followed the poet's gleam in the firm belief that

> Our echoes roll from soul to soul,
> And grow for ever and for ever.

The teacher of English, working with a class as an interpretative artist, reading for all it is worth a passage of literature, may set many echoes flying. Even as his pupils assist in the gathering of facts, they are discovering points of view for their own reflective thinking and discussion. Behind and within this whole process, however, is the teacher's personality. On him may depend to some extent the timbre of the echoes.

The main thing is the teacher's individuality. He must not be a mere bookish man, knowing human nature only from having seen it in a mirror, however great may have been the hands that held that mirror up. He must be, in the best sense of the term, a man of the world, catholic in his sympathies, broad in his views, and unprejudiced in his appreciation. He must possess some measure of that spiritual insight which makes a man conscious of an undying spirit in every manifestation of nature, and reveals to him something of the relation between things mortal and things eternal. He must be ardent and enthusiastic, with a firmly-grounded belief in the importance of his subject, and a clear vision of literature, working as a great force in the world, in harmony with all those other forces which are making for purity and righteousness.[1]

This, of course, excludes the lop-sided individuality that finds satisfaction in selfishness, self-glorification in power over others, or relief in the vain hope that "self-lessness" is possible of achievement. It implies an individuality that is the reflection of a completely integrated self, an individuality that need not, however, be free from tension, but which, when passion is sublimated to principle, may be powerful, colourful, and responsible. Without tension brains may be as dull as steel untempered, but unless intensives remain impersonal they become as blunt as mallets. It suggests, furthermore, a wholesomeness that puts to shame the meanness of cynicism and the smugness of sarcasm, a sympathy that is "unchecked by pride or scrupulous doubt", and a faith and a generosity of spirit that can surmount the four grey walls of intellectualism. Finally it assumes that the teacher has what is called "personality"—a quality which years of post-graduate study cannot give, the lack of which scholarship cannot hide, but which, when anchored in a robust body and a

[1] Roberts and Barter, *The Teaching of English*. Blackie and Son.

prudent mind, may be the expression of a resolute will and a buoyant temperament. Beyond this every teacher should develop his own working code.

Chapter Nine

CHRISTMAS EVE AT SEA

CHRISTMAS Eve ushers in the most memorable anniversary in Christendom. In every part of the Christian world people have their own special methods of celebrating the birth of Christ, and young and old in their own peculiar ways bear witness again to their faith in Christ. It is a time when the family circle draws closer to its centre, and those abroad unite in spirit with the folks at home. No one, it seems, can escape the spell, no matter where he is. It is not our situation that makes the difference, but the spirit that prevails in the hearts of men; and this fact anyone can observe who cares to examine his own experience. Here is what one poet, whose situation was most unlike our own at Christmas time, thought and felt on Christmas Eve.

(*The teacher reads the poem aloud slowly and rhythmically, giving full value to the vowels and crisp distinctness to the consonants, and letting his voice reflect the circling and ascending mood of the poem, until it reaches its climax in the fourth line of the last stanza.*)

A wind is rustling "south and soft",
   Cooing a quiet country tune,
The calm sea sighs, and far aloft
   The sails are ghostly in the moon.

Unquiet ripples lisp and purr,
   A block there pipes and chirps i' the sheave,
The wheel-ropes jar, the reef-points stir
   Faintly—and it is Christmas Eve.

The hushed sea seems to hold her breath,
   And o'er the giddy, swaying spars,
Silent and excellent as Death,
   The dim blue skies are bright with stars.

Dear God—they shone in Palestine
   Like this, and yon pale moon serene
Looked down among the lowing kine
   On Mary and the Nazarene.

The angels called from deep to deep,
   The burning heavens felt the thrill,
Startling the flocks of silly sheep
   And lonely shepherds on the hill.

To-night beneath the dripping bows
   Where flashing bubbles burst and throng,
The bow-wash murmurs and sighs and soughs
   A message from the angels' song.

The moon goes nodding down the west,
   The drowsy helmsman strikes the bell;
Rex Judaeorum natus est,
   I charge you, brothers, sing *Nowell, Nowell,*
Rex Judaeorum natus est.[1]

Where is the poet as he composes?

P. He is standing on the deck of a clipper ship far at
sea. It is dark, and as the ship rolls gently, he recollects
that this is Christmas Eve, and he feels the strangeness of
this experience of being at sea at such a time.

T. One might expect a poet far from home on
Christmas Eve to express regret or hope. What feeling
does Masefield express in this poem?

P. He imagines that the same spirit haunts the sea as
walks the land on Christmas Eve.

[1] From *Collected Poems of John Masefield.* By permission of
The Macmillan Company, publishers.

P. He wants to sing and he wishes the sailors to join with him in singing Christmas carols, just as they would if they were on land. He says

> I charge you, brothers, sing *Nowell, Nowell,*

T. Perhaps he is singing. Even this poem may be referred to as a Christmas carol. In December 1920 the first three stanzas of the poem were set to music and published as *A Christmas Carol.* If we listen attentively, we may hear the sailor-poet singing.

> A wind is rustling "south and soft",
>   Cooing a quiet country tune,
> The calm sea sighs, and far aloft
>   The sails are ghostly in the moon.

How does this song go—quickly or slowly? Sound the first line to yourselves.

P. The line moves slowly. Some of the words cannot be spoken quickly.

P. The sounds are all soft, too. You can hear the wind in words like "wind", "rustling", "south", and "soft".

T. That is true. It takes a good deal of breath to read the line properly. But why has he put quotation marks around "south and soft".

P. Perhaps he wishes to emphasize these sounds.

T. Italics would be better for emphasis. These words are quoted. What is their source?

P. They are probably quoted from the weather report in the ship's log for the night.

T. But why does he use this quoted phrase?

P. It is probably fresh in his mind from his latest entry.

P. It makes me feel that I am actually with the poet on the deck.

T. And while you stand there what sounds do you hear? Read the whole stanza aloud to give expression to the quiet melody of wind and wave.

P.

> A <u>wind</u> is <u>rustling</u> "<u>south</u> and <u>soft</u>",
>   <u>Cooing</u> a quiet country <u>tune</u>,
> The <u>calm sea sighs</u>, and <u>far aloft</u>
>   The <u>sails</u> are <u>ghostly</u> in the <u>moon</u>.

T. What effect is common to all these sounds?

P. They produce a feeling of silence as if all the forces of wind and wave were at rest.

P. They remind the poet of a "country tune", perhaps of the sound of the wind in the trees or in standing grain.

T. At any rate the effect is one of peace and hush, suggestive of a quiet countryside rather than of the usual one of a tempestuous wind howling through the rigging. We feel this hush because the poet felt it and crystallized it for us in words. His ear picked up the *voice* of this night at sea, and his eye picked out its *vision*. What does he see?

P. He sees the moonlit topsails as things "ghostly" and unreal.

T. What clue does this give to the poet's feelings?

P. He feels the eerie silence of this night at sea.

T. And what effect has this all-pervading hush and this wraith-like vision on our imaginations?

P. We feel that anything may happen.

T. The statement reveals very well our feeling of wonder and expectancy. How is this silence deepened and intensified in the next stanza?

> Unquiet ripples lisp and purr,
>   A block there pipes and chirps i' the sheave,
> The wheel-ropes jar, the reef-points stir
>   Faintly—and it is Christmas Eve.

P.P. (*A composite answer.*) Instead of the tune of the night wind singing of some far country and the sighing of the sea at rest, the sounds we now hear are short, sharp, or faint, and close at hand. The lisp and purr of ripples breaking along the sides of the ship, the piping and chirping of the ropes in the block and tackles, and the reefing points (the little ropes attached to the sail) rubbing against the sails as the ship rises and settles with the swell of the sea deepens by contrast the song of the wind and the sighing of the sea.

P. The poet, more accustomed to harsher sounds at sea, feels intensely the subdued hush produced by these faint yet "unquiet" sounds.

T. The poet is trying to capture in words the exact timbre of the sound. Now read the stanza aloud together that we may hear something of what Masefield heard.

P.P.

> *Unquiet ripples lisp and purr,*
>   *A block there pipes and chirps i' the sheave,*
> *The wheel-ropes jar, the reef-points stir*
>   *Faintly—and it is Christmas Eve.*

T. In the next stanza the poet continues to echo his impressions. Please read it so that we may hear and see and feel what this sailor-poet experienced on Christmas Eve.

P.

> *The hushed sea seems to hold her breath,*
>   *And o'er the giddy, swaying spars,*
> *Silent and excellent as Death,*
>   *The dim blue skies are bright with stars.*

T. What do you hear?

P. I hear the hush as the sea holds her breath. The whole line suggests by sound the breathless silence:

The hushed sea seems to hold her breath,

T. What is significant in the fact that the poet imagines he hears the sea holding her breath?

P. Even the sea has come under some magic spell and is waiting and expectant and holding her breath in awe of the spirit that prevails on Christmas Eve.

T. That is an excellent example of imaginative thinking. What do you see?

P. The topmasts, where they catch the moonlight, seem cut off from the ship, and at a dizzy height sway giddily against the star-studded arc of the sky.

T. To what are "the dim blue skies" compared?

P. To the silence and excellence of death.

T. That is an odd comparison, and to reveal its significance here we must first discover what the poet thinks of Death. Excel (*ex-celsus*=high) means to rise high above all others in worth or power.

P. The poet thinks of Death as the personification of a power which in its working or manifestation is silent and supreme.

T. Laurence Binyon, another modern poet, writing a lament *For the Fallen* thought of Death as something "august and royal". How did the idea of death, as a power or condition supreme and austere, get into Masefield's imagination at this time? Before you attempt to answer, read the stanza again, and try to hear and see and feel all that Masefield experienced.

P. Perhaps this perfect night with quiet sea and dim blue skies touched the poet's feelings deeply, and he could imagine nothing more wonderful and awe-inspiring than this, except death itself.

T. Sensing this strange quiet of the sea and the vastness of this sky above his ship, the poet sees the image of Death as the only analogy which can express the perfection and sublime wonder of this night called Christmas Eve. Both, to him, are "silent and excellent" and complete. But you said a moment ago that the poet's feelings were deeply touched. What proof can you find of this in what follows?

> Dear God—they shone in Palestine
> Like this, and yon pale moon serene
> Looked down among the lowing kine
> On Mary and the Nazarene.

P. He addresses God in person as a part of it all when he calls out "Dear God".

T. What forced this exclamation from him? Let us read aloud together these first four stanzas, and then the reason for his apostrophe will be very clear.

PP. (*Reading of first four stanzas.*)

T. What have you discovered? There are several reasons for this outburst of emotion.

P. The eerie stillness and strange melody of the sea fills the poet with a feeling of great peace.

P. Then, too, he feels the tension as sea and wind and sky take on subdued tones and colours in the presence of this spirit that is abroad on Christmas Eve.

PP. (*A composite answer.*) All nature stands expectant, and the poet, sensing this and wondering at the splendour and perfection of this night, is suddenly struck by its resemblance to that other night hundreds of years ago when Christ was born in Bethlehem. He imagines that on that first Christmas Eve these same bright stars and this "pale moon serene" looked down on Palestine as they must do tonight. No wonder, then, that in this spacious setting, beneath these timeless stars, he should exclaim "Dear God"!

T. But with these conditions a poet would be more likely to exclaim "Almighty God". How can you account for the epithet he uses here? Read the remainder of the stanza before answering.

P. Masefield is overwhelmed by his experience, by all that he is thinking and feeling.

T. What figures suddenly appear now in the foreground of his imagination?

P. The mother Mary and the child Jesus.

T. It may be this ancient image of Mary and Jesus, and the tender intimacy expressed in their relationship, that gives direction to the welling emotion that overflows in the poet's spontaneous cry "Dear God". And this is not all that he imagines as he thinks of that memorable night of long ago.

> The angels called from deep to deep,
>   The burning heavens felt the thrill,
> Startling the flocks of silly sheep
>   And lonely shepherds on the hill.
>
> To-night beneath the dripping bows
>   Where flashing bubbles burst and throng,
> The bow-wash murmurs and sighs and soughs
>   A message from the angels' song.

How are these two stanzas contrasted with each other?

P. In the first he imagines what took place in Palestine cn the first Christmas Eve, and in the second he describes what he hears here on this ship this Christmas Eve.

T. *There and then* is contrasted with *here and now.*
What is common to both stanzas and preserves the connection between them?

P. The angels' song is heard in both stanzas.

T. How?

P. When the angels long ago called their joy to one
another, the heavens glowed with a mysterious light that
startled the shepherds and their sheep.

T. This use of "silly" is, of course, not the modern
one. Which dictionary meaning is applicable here?

P. The word is derived from *saelig* (holy), and the
meaning appropriate here is "contented".

T. How is the angels' song heard tonight?

P. Masefield imagines he hears the angels' song in the
wash of the waves against the bow of the ship.

T. Read it aloud so that we may hear their song as the
poet imagined it.

P.

> To-night beneath the *dripping bows*
> Where *flashing bubbles burst* and *throng,*
> The *bow-wash murmurs* and *sighs* and *soughs*
> A message from the angels' *song.*

T. And what is the effect of this imagined message on
the poet?

P.

> The moon goes nodding down the west,
> The drowsy helmsman strikes the bell;
> *Rex Judaeorum natus est,*
> I charge you, brothers, sing *Nowell, Nowell,*
> *Rex Judaeorum natus est.*

The poet sings the birth of Christ as the angels sang it
long ago, and he asks his shipmates to join him in the
song *"Rex Judaeorum natus est".*

T. But he does not call them shipmates, but brothers. How can you account for this?

P. He is thinking of all men as brothers in Christ.

T. And he does not ask them but rather *charges* them to sing. Why?

P. He lays it upon them as a duty to sing, to express their faith in Christ, perhaps because he feels it so intensely himself, and wishes to share his feeling with them.

T. Yes. The drowsy helmsman hears only the bell he strikes, but Masefield hears in the eight strokes of the bell that mark the midnight hour the notes of the ancient song *"Rex Judaeorum natus est",* and he would awaken all mankind to sing. An unimaginative person would see only the moon and the stars above the Indian Ocean, hear only the drowsy wind and the creaking of the lazy ship, but the imaginative poet is suddenly stirred by this experience to a feeling of deep humility and awe. Everything that he hears and sees and feels is transformed by his imagination to express the impulse that controls him, namely the joyous desire of a seaman to memorialize in poetry the birth of Christ. What was Masefield's imaginative experience?

P. In the cooing of the soft south wind, the sighing of the sea, and the creaking of the ship, the poet imagines he hears the subdued tones of a melody that expresses the spirit of Christmas Eve. In the vision of moonlit sails moving against the vast dome of the clear night sky, the poet imagines he beholds a perfection and a magnitude that express the wonder and sublimity of the power and majesty of God. Imagining these things, he fancies he hears in the bow-wash the same angels' song that long ago set the heavens aglow with a light that drew the shepherds and the sheep to Bethlehem. The spirit of Christmas is everywhere, and everything seems charged with it. The poet feels it intensely, and sings his Christmas carol. It seems to rise from him spontaneously.

T. This is truly part of the poet's imaginative experience; his poetic experience we shall find only in the poem itself. As we read it aloud together again, we may discover the poet's and perhaps our own poetic experience in this peculiar combination of words in which thoughts, feelings, images, sounds, and rhythms are indissolubly fused.

PP. (*Reading.*)

T. This is the poetic experience of Britain's present poet laureate on a Christmas Eve at sea. If this were the only poem of Masefield's we had, what could we learn from it concerning Masefield as a seaman and a poet?

P. He is a lover of the sea, its ways and its music.

P. He can project himself imaginatively into the life of the seaman.

P. He believes in the brotherhood of men.

P. He is a Christian.

P. The qualities that appeal to me most are his sincerity and his humility.

P. He has a remarkable power to choose words for their sound and colour.

T. That is true. All the sounds and colours of this poem are in harmony. "A common greyness silvers everything" might be said of both the sounds and colours.

P. The rhythms flow easily and the rhymes are sharply contrasted. The poem sings itself.

T. The following is what one critic of Masefield said of this poem. How apt is his criticism?

The changes are rung upon realism and idyllicism. There is abrupt force of contrast; but, if aesthetic unity is sacrificed, *spiritual unity* is attained by the poem as a whole.[1]

PP. (*Discussion by the class of the terms realism, idyllicism, aesthetic unity, and spiritual unity, as applied to the poem.*)

T. If you have found profit in this poetic experience, you might like to read another poem that may some day be considered Masefield's masterpiece. *Dauber* tells the story of a boy who ran away to sea to find the secret of its beauty. It is a manly poem, made of a fibre that is coarse but sweet. Here are a few of its lines, the whole poem you may borrow from me.

> The great grey sea was running up the sky.

> Drowsed as a snail the clipper loitered south
> Slowly, with no white bone across her mouth.

> The sea was moaning and sighing and saying 'hush'.

[1] Thomas, *John Masefield.*

Chapter Ten
ANALYSIS

SOME people are of the opinion that a poem is mutilated by analysis of any kind. They suppose that the spirit of the poem perishes once the wondering mind of the reader pauses to examine the magical qualities of a passage of memorable speech. Others presume that a poem is a springboard for a plunge into a self-reflecting oration on athletics, socialism, ethics, economics, morale in a democracy, or half-baked ideas on scientific discoveries. Anything that may impair or impede the freedom of the orator is consequently wrong. Let the reader examine, for instance, any recent anthology of poetry to see how easy it is to distort many of the poems to the purposes of an extraneous propaganda. No small part of the profit to be derived from the study of poetry, as of mathematics, is found in the mental activity required in the solution of the problem—in its analysis and synthesis. The person who takes the line of least resistance, however, seldom experiences the stimulation of honest achievement.

For years we have been content to let the teacher or the preacher solve our problems for us. Now we must learn to solve our own. Whether we like it or not, we must become personally involved. The results may be surprising. There is more conviction and revelation in Herrick's brief lyric *To Daffodils,* when it is experienced, than in many a lecture on Herrick and his times. If we really care for poetry and poetic experience *Lines Composed Above Tintern Abbey* will reveal to us more of Wordsworth's spirit and its problems (and incidentally more about "schools" and "movements" and romanticism) than some lecturers can tell us. We must learn to read poetry and less about poetry. It is better to plunge with a wise companion, an experienced literary pilgrim, into Byron's *Ocean,* and therein to discover the turbulent spirit that pervades that pathetic struggle, than to listen passively to a lecturer declaim "Now we begin Byron, who was neither a great poet nor a great gentleman."

The teacher will never find out if the pupil can swim by walking with him along the bank of the river. He must see him behave in deep water, extend a helping hand in time of need, but keep him in the current until he discovers his powers. The pupil will never learn to swim sitting on the bank, listening to the exploits of famous swimmers. He must first learn to swim and then how to swim well. Part of the technique of the teacher of English is to ask the pupil such questions, from time to time, as will throw him mentally into deep water.

Minute literary criticism has been objected to on the ground that 'dissection seldom arrives at the essence of a thing because it kills it in the process.' But is this a valid objection? Does dissection ever aim at reaching the essence of a thing? Is the literal dissection practised by the biologist directed to the same end as the metaphorical dissection practised by the critic? What laboratory dissector ever thought by dissecting to explain the essence of the specimen before him? The frog lives, that is to say, functions in its specific way. But will dismembering yield up the secret of that functioning? The scientist does dissect, not to find the essence, but to examine structure, to explain the machinery. The frog he dissected is dead; whether killed in the process does not matter. But the process has not been entirely destructive because the dead frog has enabled him to understand better the living frog and ultimately all life.

Literal dissection is concerned with types, with the universal. Criticism is dealing with individual works of art. The killing of a work of art may evoke lament as the killing of the biologist's frog will not, because the one killing is indirectly constructive, the other sheer murder. But it is to be doubted whether a work of art can be killed by metaphorical dissection. A picture may be slashed to pieces, a marble shivered, but that presumably is not dissection. A poem or a piece of music cannot be killed even in this way (because it is essentially intangible, whereas the plastic arts depend upon physical media for their communicability). Conversely it is doubtful whether a work of art which is 'killed' by criticism ever was a work of art. A poem must stand looking into (always provided that due sympathy is shown for the poet's intention). Whole and parts must be sound. The appreciation of detail and general impression are complementary parts of the appreciation of the whole. Criticism will reveal works of apparently perfect technique which lack life and works which are momentary illusion and nothing else. On the other hand criticism illustrates the truth of the adage 'To him that hath shall be given'; a good work of art will gain in meaning under criticism. The minute study of Rubens' brushwork, of character-drawing in Sophocles, of vowel-sounds and proportions, all help not distract, provided that our final view is that of the work as a whole. A motor-car engine, to function well, requires occasional dissection as well as running; but only a fool would complain that he could not take the engine to pieces while it is in action.[1]

Some teachers teach too much. In fact they teach so much of the time that neither they nor their pupils have time for reflection. Like a house full of active inmates, the mind needs a little time to put things right. This does not mean a slackening of activity when intensive work is being done, but an opportunity to evaluate the work that has been done.

Throughout a year's work in English not all the study is made as intensive as that which has been illustrated here. At the beginning of each year in any grade intensive work should be the order of the day; and it should

[1] R. W. Moore, *Idea and Expression*. G. Bell & Sons, 1937. By permission of the author and the publishers.

be continued until the pupils are familiar with the methods of study and the advantages to be derived from them. After the pupils have learned how to penetrate to the heart of experience that throbs within the art of a poem, they should be encouraged to put forth with a few suggestions and, under judicious supervision, to make their own discoveries. A well-trained class, given time to contemplate the matter, will present, orally or in writing, interesting and valuable reflections on the suitability of form to substance in a poem like de la Mare's *The Scribe* after a few minutes of teaching of it has revealed that God and man possess some secret that defies analysis or description. Or, instead of teaching the poem at all, the teacher allows time for the class to discover what proof can be found in *The Scribe* of de la Mare's awe and wonder at the power and mystery of God.

Some poems require more intensive treatment than others. *County Guy* and *Proud Maisie* together can be taught in half the time that it takes to teach *Of Old Sat Freedom on the Heights.*

The best and most effective introduction for a lesson on *Bonnie Dundee* or *Caller Herrin'* or *Trade Winds* is the singing of the poem by the class.

The examination of a good parody on *Cargoes* quickly reveals the characteristic effects of that collection of rhythmic images. There is an advantage in the use of parody here.

In the teaching of English the opportunities for the exercise of initiative and imagination are endless. To know when and how to prepare the way for reflection, however, requires insight, skill, and good judgment.

Chapter Eleven

THE POOL

Come with me, follow me, swift as a moth,
Ere the wood-doves waken.
Lift the long leaves and look down, look down
Where the light is shaken,
Amber and brown,
On the woven ivory roots of the reed,
On a floating flower and a weft of weed
And a feather of froth.

Here in the night all wonders are,
Lapped in the lift of the ripple's swing,—
A silver shell and a shaken star,
And a white moth's wing.
Here the young moon when the mists unclose
Swims like the bud of a golden rose.

I would live like an elf where the wild grapes cling,
I would chase the thrush
From the red rose-berries.
All the day long I would laugh and sing
With the black choke-cherries.

I would shake the bees from the milkweed blooms,
And cool, O cool,
Night after night I would leap in the pool,
And sleep with the fish in the roots of the rush.
Clear, O clear my dreams should be made
Of emerald light and amber shade,
Of silver shallows and golden glooms.
Sweet, O sweet my dreams should be
As the dark sweet water enfolding me
Safe as a blind shell under the sea.[1]

[1] From *The Complete Poems of Marjorie Pickthall*. By permission of the publishers, McClelland and Stewart Limited.

189

T. In what mood or state of mind is the writer?

PP. (*After reading the poem silently, the pupils answer in turn, and the teacher collects the material on the blackboard.*) Her mood is carefree. Adventurous. Joyous. Fanciful. Excited. Imaginative. Wishful. Ecstatic. Lively. Yearning.

T. These words are all more or less applicable, but since they express ideas that may be classified under two general headings, we may find the writer's mood in a combination of two of them, such as imaginative adventure or fanciful wishing.

> Come with me, follow me, swift as a moth,
> Ere the wood-doves waken.
> Lift the long leaves and look down, look down
> Where the light is shaken,
> Amber and brown,
> On the woven ivory roots of the reed,
> On a floating flower and a weft of weed
> And a feather of froth.

T. Who is invited to go with her?

P. Everyone.

T. Where are we invited to go?

P. To the pool.

T. How?

P. As "swift as a moth".

T. When?

P. Before dawn, "Ere the wood-doves waken".

T.

> Come with me, follow me, swift as a moth,
> Ere the wood-doves waken.

What gives a feeling of urgency to these lines?

P. The spontaneity of the phrasing, the time-limit set, and the need for speed all suggest an urgency.

T. How is this effect suggested by the rhythm?

P.

> / ‿ ‿ / ‿ ‿ / ‿ ‿ /
> Come with me | follow me, | swift as | a moth |
> ‿ ‿ / — /
> Ere the wood | doves wak(en).

The variety and irregularity of metres is consistent with the tumbled haste of the statement.

T. How is this effect continued in the next line?

P.

> / ‿ — / ‿ ‿ / ‿ /
> Lift the | long leaves | and look down, | look down |

The same effect is secured by the irregularity of metre to suit the feeling and by the repetition of "look down".

T. Why the urgency? What are we to see?

P. We must go quickly and early if we wish to see the light, amber and brown, shaken on the ivory roots, the floating flower, the weft of weed, and the feather of froth.

T. What quality is common to all these images?

P. They are all delicate and fragile, even the light is shaken, the flower floating, and the froth feathery.

T. In how many other ways is this airy-fairy quality secured?

P. The sounds are light; the harmony of vowels and consonants and the alliteration give a feathery breath-like quality to the words.

P. The colours amber and ivory may suggest a fairy delicacy of tone.

P. The rhythm, too, is as light and wavering as the imagery.

T. What is contributed by the form?

P. The form of the stanza is irregular; so is the rhyme scheme. Both the rhythm and the rhyme are in keeping with the whim of the writer, with her lively and fanciful mood. They reinforce it.

T.

> Here in the night all wonders are,
> Lapped in the lift of the ripple's swing,—
> A silver shell and a shaken star,
> And a white moth's wing.
> Here the young moon when the mists unclose
> Swims like the bud of a golden rose.

What is the chief point of contrast between this and the previous stanza?

P. In the first stanza we "Lift the long leaves and look down" into the secluded pool at dawn, but in the second "Here in the night all wonders are."

T. What are some of the wonders to be seen when the "mists unclose"?

P. A shell, a star, a white moth's wing, and the young moon; and again there are no harsh contrasts of colour.

T. Where are these objects seen?

P. In the pool.

T. Yes, but where in the pool are they seen?

P. "Lapped in the lift of the ripple's swing."

T. This is fanciful, indeed. What other proof can you find that the writer is indulging her imagination?

P. The shell is not white nor grey, but silver; the star is not firmly fixed, but shaken; and the reflection of the young moon "*swims* like the *bud* of a *golden* rose".

P. The lilt of the rhythm and the firm effect of the rhyming couplet following quickly upon the contrasting rhymes, reflect her imaginative mood.

T.

> I would live like an elf where the wild grapes cling,
> I would chase the thrush
> From the red rose-berries.
> All the day long I would laugh and sing
> With the black choke-cherries.

What indication is there that the writer's point of view has changed with this stanza?

P. Previously the writer has been our observant and imaginative companion, but now, forgetting us, she wishes to flit through the air as an elf. It may take some speed to keep up with her.

T. What proof can you find that she is possessed of a spirit of complete abandon?

P. She wishes to spend the whole day chasing the thrush and laughing and singing.

P. Even the rhythm chuckles a little in the line "With the black choke-cherries".

P. The rhythm of the first line is as spacious and free as her mood

> ⌣ ⌣ / ⌣ ⌣ / ⌣ ⌣ / — /
> I would live | like an elf | where the wild | grapes cling

T. How can you account for the fact that this stanza has only two tetrametre lines, although the previous stanza has five?

PP. (*A composite answer.*) In the second stanza the regularity of line length is consistent with the concentrated effect of the imagery. The dimetre lines in the third stanza point the thrusts of her short imaginative flights.

T. A rhyme in stanza two is carried forward to stanza three. What is gained by this?

P. It helps to preserve the unity of the poem and its mood at a time when both are in danger of being broken.

T.

> I would shake the bees from the milkweed blooms,
> And cool, O cool,
> Night after night I would leap in the pool,
> And sleep with the fish in the roots of the rush.
> Clear, O clear my dreams should be made
> Of emerald light and amber shade,
> Of silver shallows and golden glooms.
> Sweet, O sweet my dreams should be
> As the dark sweet water enfolding me
> Safe as a blind shell under the sea.

How is the sequence of thought and feeling preserved with the previous stanza?

P. The first line here continues in the same vein.

P. At least one rhyme in stanza three finds its completion in this one.

T. How would she spend her nights?

P. She would "sleep with the fish in the roots of the rush" and dream of lights and shadows, the fairy colours green and amber, silver and golden, caught from her surroundings.

T. The previous stanza suggests the hot excitement of her day-long chase. What contrasts with that in this stanza?

P. Here she finds cool relief and refreshment.

T. What other qualities will her dreams possess?

P. They will be clear and sweet and undisturbed.

T. To what state has this flight of fancy brought her?

P. Like a "blind shell under the sea" she is unconscious of everything—even of physical sensation. Her state is now reduced to that of one of the lowest forms of life.

P. Her satisfaction is now complete; and the long stanza, the regular line length, and the triple rhyme with which the poem closes reinforce this effect.

P. She is now secluded from the world from which she wished to escape.

T. Is her experience one of *escape* or of *quest?*

P. There is not even a suggestion that she is escaping from anything.

P. But in the first line she invites the world and his friend to go with her.

T. Well, what experience has she left crystallized in the words of the poem?

P. Certainly there is here some of the spontaneous delight and freedom of fancy that she imagines an elf may enjoy.

P. There is, too, some of the thrill of discovery as she projects herself in imagination into the fanciful life of an elf-like creature.

T. What support can you find in the form of the poem for these opinions?

P. The stanza form varies with her whim. The length of the stanzas and the choice between dimetres and tetrametres vary with her changing point of view. But some formal unity is preserved by interweaving some of the rhymes of the last three stanzas.

P. The form and the substance fit each other. Even the sounds and suggestions of the words are in harmony with the imagery and the rhythm. The poem preserves an imaginative experience in permanent form.

T. This poem appeared first in the *Metropolitan Magazine* in October 1907. In a paragraph, present the reasons (based on the poem) which, you think, led the editor to publish the poem. Assume that the editor admired J. S. Mill's dictum: poetry is "the product of man's imagination set in motion by his feelings".

Notes and Comments on the Teaching of *The Pool*

It is easy to imagine what a sentimentalist would do with this poem. It is a waste of time to romance before a high school class about the divine elation of poetry, the inspiration of the imagination, the rangy flight of a poet's spirit, or the beauties of nature. Not only is it wasteful; it is positively harmful. If the pupil does not realize at once that the writer of this poem had acute powers of observation and a lively fancy, no amount of effervescence from pools I have seen or Seven Dwarfs I have met will do him any good. Omit the harangue on verse, free or otherwise, and concentrate on the poem and its poetry. Follow the poet closely and the poem will teach itself, provide its own background, and create its own emotional atmosphere. If the teacher sees the images, hears the sounds, and feels the rhythm, it is a simple and pleasant exercise to lead the pupils to discover an experience that resembles in some degree the poet's experience.

If the teacher is content merely to select the "pictures", collect the figures of speech, construct the rhyme scheme, and choose the most "beautiful" or most "musical" stanza, then the poem as a literary experience will not pass through the mind of the pupil, but across it. Unless the poetic elements of the poem are integrated with the central experience they create, it is better to leave them untouched and let the class read and read and read the poem.

It is likewise harmful to indulge in a long argument on escapism at the end of the study. The best the teacher can do is (1) to clarify one opinion and let the pupils accept it, or reject it if they can find support for a better one of their own; (2) follow the order laid down by the poet in the sequence of the poem so that extraneous thoughts, feelings, and images are not allowed to impair the unity and intensity of the reader's poetic experience; and (3) integrate all the poetic elements in the poem in such a way that poetry is preserved in the art of the poem.

Chapter Twelve

A THUNDERSTORM

T. You have all experienced at some time the effects of a thunderstorm, and the mere mention of the word should awaken feelings of varying kinds.

What interest might a student of electricity find in a thunderstorm? Or a student of weather conditions? Or a landscape artist?

PP. (*Brief class discussion.*)

T. These reactions are not identical with our own, but they present new points of view. What a poet might see in a thunderstorm might be quite arresting. *A Thunderstorm* by Emily Dickinson, gives one reaction: read it please.

PP. (*Pupils read silently.*)

T. Who will volunteer to read this poem aloud? (*Pupil reads.*)

> The wind begun to rock the grass
> With threatening tunes and low,—
> He flung a menace at the earth,
> A menace at the sky.
>
> The leaves unhooked themselves from trees
> And started all abroad;
> The dust did scoop itself like hands
> And throw away the road.
>
> The wagons quickened on the streets,
> The thunder hurried slow;
> The lightning showed a yellow beak,
> And then a livid claw.

The birds put up the bars to nests,
The cattle fled to barns;
There came one drop of giant rain,
And then, as if the hands

That held the dams had parted hold,
The waters wrecked the sky,
But overlooked my father's house,
Just quartering a tree.[1]

T. What did this writer see in a thunderstorm that interested her?

P. She saw the thunderstorm in the form of a monstrous creature threatening the earth.

T.

The wind begun to rock the grass
With threatening tunes and low,—
He flung a menace at the earth,
A menace at the sky.

What first attracted her attention?

P. The effect of the wind on the grass is given in the first line,

The wind begun to rock the grass

T. What is unusual in the way that is stated?

P. We should say, "The wind began", or "had begun", or "having begun".

T. Why did the writer express it this way?

P. It may be that she wished to express the sound of the wind. "Beg*un*" expresses the rumble of a strong wind better than "beg*an*". It also expresses the suddenness of the first warning.

[1] From *The Poems of Emily Dickinson*, edited by Martha Dickinson Bianchi and Alfred Leete Hampson. Reprinted by permission of Little, Brown & Company.

T. "Tune" is an odd word to use in this connection. How can you justify it?

P. Perhaps, the sound of the wind is in harmony with the evil thing that threatens.

T. To what does "He" refer?

P. To the thunderstorm, as she imagines its form to be.

T. What is the purpose and effect of this personification?

P. The thunderstorm is not just a natural phenomenon to the writer, but an evil creature threatening everything in its path.

T. It may be that she sees this thunderstorm as Boanerges, one of the "sons of tumult". In the first line the wind is seen in its effect on the grass. What form would this "menace", flung at earth and sky, take?

P. The menace may be seen in the form of thunder clouds, like mighty wings, with their heavy shadows, driven before the storm.

T. You might expect the second and fourth lines to rhyme. What is the effect of throwing against each other, opposite extremes of sound as in "low" and "sky"?

P. It is in keeping with the thundering tone and imagery of the whole stanza.

T. It has been said of Emily Dickinson: "She juggled with words as one might play with unset gems, more for sheer joy of them than adaptation to her own emergency, until one set at a peculiar angle of her line told her by a flash that it was hers." And again: "Her spontaneity in words pries under accepted usage or sets fire to it."

What instances of her spontaneity and insight in the use of words have you already found?

(Discussion to recapitulate substance and style of stanza.)

T. We shall see if this is characteristic of the poem as a whole. Read the second stanza aloud.

P. (Pupil reads.)

T. What is unusual in the first line?

P. The writer attributes power to the leaves that they do not possess.

T. With what effect?

P. They are not blown off the branches, but unhook themselves from trees. They are all seen to leave the trees at an instant as if electrified by fear.

T. How is that borne out by the next line?

P. "All abroad" suggests that they are like creatures panic-stricken and flying aimlessly.

T. Emily Dickinson has been commended for her "acute sensitiveness of perception" and her "gnomic imagery". What is unusual and quaint in the way she interprets what she sees in the next two lines?

P. Normally we might see a strong wind blow a road-surface away in handfuls, but the writer sees the dust, suddenly alive, fleeing to escape the storm.

T. What purpose is served by these two images?

P. They intensify the fear that is awakened by an electric storm.

T. How is this effect sustained and increased in the next stanza, first line? *(Pupil reads stanza aloud.)*

P. The wagons *quickened* as if alive and anxious in their haste.

T. What is the effect of "The thunder hurried slow"?

P. The thunder was coming nearer and nearer in its own unhurrying haste. It forewarned of a monster that would inevitably arrive and was inescapable.

P. Is "hurried slow" good grammar?

T. Why would you object to it?

P. It should be *hurried slowly. Slow* is an adjective.

T. Why did the writer use this old form of the adverb here?

P. Its sound and the emphasis it attracts best convey the impression of the thunder and the deliberate speed of its approach.

T. Other examples of this figure of speech, called *oxymoron,* are found in the following statements:

And faith unfaithful kept him falsely true.

He was engaged in perpetuating the busy idleness of the world.

(Poetic licence is a privilege of poets, but not of pupils.)

T. What feeling do the following images awaken?

> The lightning showed a yellow beak
> And then a livid claw.

P. Fear.

T. What do they tell you concerning the nature of the "He" in the first stanza?

P. The writer sees the thunderstorm as a monstrous bird-like creature, prepared to rend, ravage, and destroy.

T. What is the difference in colour between the beak and the claw?

P. The beak shows the bright yellow of forked lightning, and the claw the bluish leaden colour that follows the yellow as the bolt strikes the earth.

T. In stanzas 2 and 3 the second and fourth lines do not rhyme; nor do their sounds contrast with each other. What is the purpose and effect of these "near-rhymes" or "half-rhymes" as they are sometimes called?

P. There is enough similarity of sound to bind the stanza into a structural unit. There is enough difference to keep an ear accustomed to rhyme expectant and suspended.

T. How is this effect of "off tones" in keeping with the theme?

P. It is in keeping with the writer's weird impression of the storm and the fearful things she imagines.

T. Now, let us see what the next step is in the progress of the storm! Read the next two stanzas in such a way as to express the tension and suspense that is felt. Pause at the end of the fourth stanza to indicate the form, but carry the thought and feeling forward to stanza five by retaining the same pitch.

(*Pupil reads.*)

T. How would birds "put up the bars to nests"?

P. By sitting on their nests to protect them.

T. Then, why did the writer not say so? What else was she trying to express?

P. Perhaps she was trying to express the helplessness and futility of birds and cattle to escape or to ward off the ferocity of this threatening creature.

T. Why does the writer allot a whole line to a single "giant" raindrop?

P. It contrasts with the dryness which precedes it and the flood that immediately follows.

P. It increases the tension and suspense that was awakened earlier. The use of the word "giant" is in keeping with the theme.

T. In the line "The waters *wrecked* the sky" the storm seems to have reached its climax. Everything is suddenly blotted out. Impressions are confused. What are the stages by which the storm reached this blackout?

(*Discussion of the theme and its development.*)

T. What other factors contribute to the unity of this work of art?

P. It is an imaginative unit in the writer's mind. She never loses sight of the thunderstorm as a monster of some kind.

P. It is an emotional unit also because throughout she regards the thunderstorm as a fearsome thing.

T. There is another factor that seems to clinch the whole matter. What is the time-relation of the last two lines to all that precedes them?

P. The last two lines suggest that the storm is over. The previous lines tell of its approach.

P. The last two lines suggest calm and relief after the storm.

P. The writer's imagination is now at rest and she records a fact, namely that a bolt of lightning missed the house but split a neighbouring tree four ways.

T. What is the implied or imaginary subject of the verb "overlooked"?

P. The subject is *He,* the monster attended by wind, fire, and flood, and to which the writer directed our attention in the first stanza.

T. What is the grammatical relation of the last line to the line that precedes it?

P. It modifies the implied subject of the verb "overlooked".

T. What is attributed to this monster in the word "just"?

P. "Just" suggests the nice precision with which this creature can use its weird, uncanny power and exercise choices that are apparently fantastic.

T. Excitement has given place to calm. To what in the writer's mind has fear given place?

P. To wonder and awe.

T. At what?

P. She may wonder what power released this storm upon the earth and she may stand in awe of the strange "other-world" intelligence that directs its course.

T. What is the artistic significance of the rhyme-irregularity in "sky" and "tree"?

P. It helps to bring out sharply her wistfulness, her desire to understand what is not given us to know.

T. Which is more profound and affecting for her, the *fear* that preceded or the *wonder* that followed the havoc wrought by the storm?

(*Discussion follows.*)

T. Of the art of poetry, Emily Dickinson once said, "too much of proof affronts belief." What proof can you find of her ability to practise her belief? (A recapitulation follows in which details of substance and of structure are examined in the light of the whole impression. Opinions are supported by quotations and statements such as the following:

—"Her entities were vast as her words were few."

—"She never hesitated to take the unprecedented leap, and land solid on the air."

—"Nothing was ever terse enough for her."

—"Her loyalty was to aesthetic impression rather than to rhyme or grammar."

—"She drew off the essence of an experience and then watched delighted while it crystallized in words until finally it formed a miniature of poetic art as sharply lined, as delicate, and as tenuous as a snowflake.")

T. Why is a poet's record of a thunderstorm likely to be more interesting than that of a weather-man?

(*Discussion.*)

(*The poem is read aloud by the whole class.*)

(*A collection of Emily Dickinson's poems is recommended for supplementary reading.*)

N.B. After D. C. Scott's poem *A Summer Storm,* p. 339, *Shorter Poems,* had been studied independently, it might be contrasted briefly with *A Thunderstorm,* perhaps with detriment to both poems since their words and methods are not alike and they are in no sense competitors.

Chapter Thirteen

SIR PATRICK SPENS[1]

T. Story telling is one of the oldest of the arts. Thousands of years ago, one can well believe, people listened with interest to stories of heroes and their strange exploits. There is abundant evidence that our early ancestors not only listened to stories in song but also joined in the singing or chanting. Song, apparently, has always come easily and naturally to the lips of British peoples. In peace or war their moods have been reflected in their songs and stories, and one of the finest collections of folk songs in the world is British.

Today we are going to read a story in verse to which men listened hundreds of years ago. At their feasts or in their communal halls they heard it recited or chanted, sometimes to the accompaniment of the harp, but to the people in that early listening time it meant much more than any song or story could possibly mean to people today. It was story, drama, song, and even news, all in one. Today we have, for better or for worse, movies, radios, libraries, and newspapers, but our early ancestors in Great Britain in the 14th and 15th centuries had little more than stories and ballads like *Sir Patrick Spens.*

> The king sits in Dumferling toune,
>   Drinking the blude-reid wine:
> "O whar will I get guid sailor,
>   To sail this schip of mine?"

[1] Pronounced Spence.

Up and spak an eldern knicht,
  Sat at the king's richt kne:
"Sir Patrick Spence is the best sailor
  That sails upon the se."

The king has written a braid letter,
  And signd it wi his hand,
And sent it to Sir Patrick Spence,
  Was walking on the sand.

The first line that Sir Patrick red,
  A loud lauch lauched he;
The next line that Sir Patrick red,
  The teir blinded his ee.

"O wha is this has don this deid,
  This ill deid don to me,
To send me out this time o' the yeir,
  To sail upon the se!

"Mak hast, mak hast, my mirry men all,
  Our guid schip sails the morne:"
"O say na sae, my master deir,
  For I feir a deadlie storme.

"Late late yestreen I saw the new moone,
  Wi the auld moone in hir arme,
And I feir, I feir, my deir master,
  That we will cum to harme."

O our Scots nobles wer richt laith
  To weet their cork-heild schoone;
Bot lang owre a' the play wer playd,
  Thair hats they swam aboone.

O lang, lang may their ladies sit,
  Wi thair fans into their hand,
Or eir they se Sir Patrick Spence
  Cum sailing to the land.

O lang, lang may the ladies stand,
  Wi thair gold kems in their hair,
Waiting for thair ain deir lords,
  For they'll se thame na mair.

> Haf owre, haf owre to Aberdour,
>   It's fiftie fadom deip,
> And thair lies guid Sir Patrick Spence,
>   Wi the Scots lords at his feit.

What are your first impressions on hearing this ballad read?

P. It is an exciting story, and its language makes it sound as if it really happened.

P. It is told in a vigorous manner. Only the bare facts are given.

P. The rhythm is swift and strong.

T. What is the chief incident of the story?

P. A ship is lost at sea with all hands on board.

T. In another version of this story some of the details are given of the wreck of the ship in a storm. Who is the chief character in the story?

P. Sir Patrick Spens.

T. Of what country is he a knight?

P. Scotland.

T. How do you know?

P. The language is Scottish; Scots nobles were on board the ship; and I believe Dumferling is in Scotland.

T. Yes, Dumferling is a town in Scotland, situated about five miles inland from the seaport of Aberdour on the north shore of the Firth of Forth. In the thirteenth century Dumferling was the seat of the Scottish kings.

> The king sits in Dumferling toune,
>   Drinking the blude-reid wine:
> "O whar will I get guid sailor,
>   To sail this schip of mine?"

How does this beginning contrast with that of a modern story?

P. There is no attempt here to give a "build-up", to arouse interest.

P. We are thrust into the presence of a king, where the first scene of the drama has already begun.

T. What is taking place?

P. The king is drinking "the blude-reid wine". He may be carousing with his knights. More than that we do not know.

T. What qualities of character would you attribute to the king from his manner of speech?

P. He appears to be a bluff and hearty fellow.

T. If this story appealed to people hundreds of years ago, what may we deduce were some of their interests?

P. They were interested in the king and his court. Here they would not only see the king, but hear him speak. They would wonder, as we do, who the good sailor is, and why the king's ship is to sail.

P. They must have been imaginative. A few facts, strong character, and bold action sufficed. A few hints were enough. They were content to provide a suitable "atmosphere", if some stark and clearly drawn outlines were provided. They were interested in life, and they wanted it raw.

T. How can you show that the structure of the poem or of the stanza is in harmony with these facts?

P. The rhythm is strong and swift and definite like the rhythm of speech, and the rhymes are clear and bold. No time is wasted on moody introductions. If the lines were startlingly abrupt, so much the better.

T.

> Up and spak an eldern knicht,
>   Sat at the kings richt kne:
> "Sir Patrick Spence is the best sailor
>   That sails upon the se."

What information is given here on the nature of the meeting?

P. Apparently it is a state meeting of the king and his counsellors. The knights are sitting in order of seniority, and the eldest knight proclaims Sir Patrick Spence the best sailor.

T.

> The king has written a braid letter,
>   And signd it wi his hand,
> And sent it to Sir Patrick Spence,
>   Was walking on the sand.

What contrast in situation is given here?

P. In the first line of the stanza we see the king and his court at Dumferling, but in the last line we see Sir Patrick Spens walking on the sand, perhaps at Aberdour.

T. Why, do you suppose, is he not at court with the other knights?

P. He is probably awaiting a command from the king.

P. It is more likely that he is not a politician but a sailor, and would prefer to be beside his ship.

T. Why would this stanza appeal to our early listening ancestors?

P. The sudden and abrupt jump in the narrative from one place to another as the action sweeps onward at a headlong pace would interest them as it interests us. They were more concerned with essential facts than with artistic sequence.

P. They would see the dramatic acts of the king as he orders his scribe to make a letter, and as he on it places his personal seal.

T. It seems pointless to think of a "braid letter" as a long letter. What kind of letter would it be?

P. It was probably a large official scroll on which the letters stood out in bold relief.

T.

> The first line that Sir Patrick red,
> A loud lauch lauched he;
> The next line that Sir Patrick red,
> The teir blinded his ee.

What would interest listeners in this stanza?

P. The sudden change of emotion from laughing to weeping would interest anyone. Even we wish to know what made Sir Patrick laugh so heartily as he does in the line "A loud lauch lauched he."

T. Why do you think he laughed?

P. He may have laughed at the manner of the king's greeting.

T. A stanza from another version of this poem in its oldest form may throw light on this point.

"To Noroway, to Noroway, to Noroway o'er the faem;
The king's daughter o' Noroway, 'tis thou must bring her hame."

There was at this time, we are told, a Scottish act of parliament which forbade vessels to put to sea in the winter season on account of the number of ships that had been lost in storms. Sir Patrick may have laughed, indeed, at the king's good jest until he read on to discover that this

was a command addressed to himself; but, then, any guess
may be a good one on this point, as it may likewise be on
the purpose of the mission to Norway. It may be that the
Scottish king wished his granddaughter, Princess Margaret
of Norway, to be brought to Scotland to wed the son of
the English king. To formulate such plans the king may
have called his counsellors together. History on this point
is somewhat dim. The reactions of Sir Patrick, however,
remain clear and honest enough!

> O wha is this has don this deid,
>   This ill deid don to me,
> To send me out this time o' the yeir,
>   To sail upon the se!

What is his first reaction after reading the letter?

P. He suspects that someone at court bears him ill will,
and wishes to send him out to certain death at sea. What
does he prepare to do?

P.

> "Make hast, mak hast, my mirry men all,
>   Our guid schip sails the morne:"
> "O say na sae, my master deir,
>   For I feir a deadlie storme.
>
> "Late late yestreen I saw the new moone,
>   Wi the aulde moone in hir arme,
> And I feir, I feir, my deir master,
>   That we will cum to harme."

T. What is Sir Patrick's second reaction?

P. He obeys the command of the king and prepares to
set sail at once, perhaps before the weather turns rough.

T. What objection is raised?

P. A sailor pleads with him not to set out when all
signs point to a "deadlie storme", but it is evident from
what follows that Sir Patrick put to sea at once.

T. Why would these stanzas interest the people who heard them first?

P. They resemble the speeches of men under the stress of emotion in the drama of real life. The natural belief of early peoples in signs and omens would echo the sailor's reading of the moon. It would excite .them with fear because they would understand at once how reasonable was the sailor's fear.

T.

> O our Scots nobles were richt laith
>   To weet their cork-heild schoone;
> Bot lang owre a' the play were playd,
>   Thair hats they swam aboone.

Why were there nobles on board this ship?

P. If this was a royal mission to Norway, these nobles would form the official guard for the return of the king's granddaughter.

T. What sort of men were they?

P. They were certainly not sailors because they were loath to get their cork-heeled shoes wet. They were probably courtiers, who looked with disdain upon the rough and ready life of seamen.

T. What is the effect of the contrast in this stanza?

P. It emphasizes the unexpected change in condition and mood. The suddenness of the change shows how callously these early listeners accepted disaster and death.

T. At least in the telling this is true. The expression of primitive emotions was neither bold nor strange, but rather commonplace and natural to them.

> O lang, lang may their ladies sit,
>   Wi their fans into thair hand,
> Or eir they se Sir Patrick Spence
>   Cum sailing to the land.

Again the story is shunted abruptly forward. Where are we now?

P. We see the ladies sitting in their bower.

T. What are they doing?

P. They are waiting for Sir Patrick to bring the courtiers and their royal charge to land.

T. Why has the balladist presented them with fans in their hands?

P. The fan was a sign of the coquette; it expressed some of the language of love. The ladies flirt their fans in anticipation of their lords' return.

T. What bitter thought is suggested by this situation?

P. We know that these ladies will never see again the lords whose admiration they invite.

T. Read the next stanza, and state how it contrasts with the one just read.

P.

> O lang, lang may the ladies stand,
>   Wi thair gold kems in thair hair,
> Waiting for thair ain deir lords,
>   For they'll se thame na mair.

Some time has apparently elapsed since the action suggested in the previous stanza, and the ladies are now seen standing, perhaps on the shore, anxiously hoping that their lords will eventually return to them safely.

T. What is the effect of so much repetition of language?

P. These people liked language and the repetition of sounds; they liked to hear words ring.

P. It accentuates the contrast of essential details. Our attention, for instance, is directed now to their gold combs rather than to their fans.

T. I wonder why?

P. We know that these precious ornaments will soon give place to mourning attire, and our sympathy for the ladies is awakened by the sharp contrasts and the restraint of bare details.

T.

> Haf owre, haf owre to Aberdour,
>   It's fiftie fadom deip,
> And thair lies guid Sir Patrick Spence,
>   Wi the Scots lords at his feit.

To what extent is there poetic justice in this ending?

P. If these nobles had anything to do with the king's choice of Sir Patrick, they have received their deserts.

P. Even in death these nobles are still placed beneath Sir Patrick in station.

T. Why is he called "guid Sir Patrick Spens"? Are we to believe that he was the type of man who had never said "damn" to his first mate?

P. The people remembered him for his worth and courage and obedience. A heroic character, he probably represented their ideal of common nobility.

T. This ballad ends as abruptly as it began. Please read it aloud to express what it means to you.

P. (*Pupil reads. Then the class may read in concert.*)

T. Coleridge, the author of the celebrated poem *The Rime of the Ancient Mariner* which we studied last year, once said of this poem: "A grand old ballad, Sir Patrick Spens!" Why did this poem appeal to him?

P. It tells a good story in an interesting way. These are the plain unvarnished facts and the reader can take them or leave them. Much is left to the reader's imagination and power of feeling.

P. The story is swift and sure of foot. It is forthright and downright, and rugged in both thought and feeling; there is no stumbling or shuffling about in false sentiment.

T. And one might add—or in literary craft, "It tells itself."

P. Coleridge would find in this poem the thrill of adventure, the tang of the sea, and the speech rhythms of a people. He would see that every word fits easily and naturally in its allotted place.

T. He would see, too, that rhymes are a help and not a hindrance, that these early listening folk had an appreciation of the art of repetition and of omission. They were brave and honest enough to trust their ears. Coleridge doubtless saw at once that this "grand old ballad, Sir Patrick Spens" was not a literary hybrid but one of the wild flowers of English verse.

Notes and Comments on the Teaching of *Sir Patrick Spens*

This is not the only way to introduce this poem. It is sometimes better to let a ballad introduce itself by reading it aloud to the class. The chief reason for the introduction given above is to invite the class to listen as they imagine people hundreds of years ago listened, and to see the poem as a whole and in detail from that imaginary point of view.

When the reading of any narrative poem is complete, it is a good plan to see that the pupils have a fairly clear idea of the story, the incident, or the character. This is the purpose of the general analysis.

The aim of the detailed study is to lead the pupils to a deeper understanding, to hear and see and feel the ballad as a poem taken from those pages of Britain's literary scrap-book devoted to the childhood of English poetry. The aim is not to collect the characteristics of a ballad either during or at the end of the study of the poem, but rather to discover the effect produced by any characteristics peculiar to the ballad at the time when they occur in the sequence. The study of the technique of a modern literary, or artistic, ballad is quite a different matter, as we shall see later. In the old popular ballads these characteristics were not detached but closely integrated parts of the whole, and were as natural to the expression as the language, the grammar, and the spelling. If the rough and ready manner of expression and the rugged elemental emotions portrayed are sacrificed to the zeal of the collector of balladistic devices, all is lost.

There are, of course, other ways to conclude the study of the popular ballad. Since it is oral poetry, it should be read aloud. Such questions as, Why are they still popularly read? or, To what do they owe their appeal today? may serve as well as the one used in this lesson to synthesize the study of the poem and to invite the class to look at the poem as a whole from the historical rather than the literary point of view.

If explanatory, historical material is required for the clarifying of some fact, it should be introduced when the need for it arises.

Advanced classes are sometimes interested in other versions of this ballad and in trying to "date" the poem by such expressions as *cork-heild, play,* etc., but an original good reading of the poem by the teacher is, without a doubt, the most important single feature of a successful lesson on *Sir Patrick Spens.*

Chapter Fourteen

BENEDICTUS

THIS lesson should begin with the reading of the whole of
Chapter I of the Gospel according to St. Luke. The
facts as given there are easier to understand than they are
in any paraphrase of the chapter. It is preferable to have
the pupils bring their Bibles to class. After the reading of
the chapter has been completed, the pupils should be given
time for silent and oral reading.

Blessed be the Lord God of Israel;
for he hath visited and redeemed his people,
And hath raised up an horn of salvation for us
in the house of his servant David;
As he spoke by the mouth of his holy prophets,
which have been since the world began:
That we should be saved from our enemies,
and from the hand of all that hate us;
To perform the mercy promised to our fathers,
and to remember his holy covenant;
The oath which he sware to our father Abraham,
That he would grant unto us, that we being delivered
out of the hand of our enemies
might serve him without fear,
In holiness and righteousness before him,
all the days of our life.
And thou, child, shalt be called the prophet of the Highest:
for thou shalt go before the face of the Lord to prepare his ways;
To give knowledge of salvation unto his people
by the remission of their sins,
Through the tender mercy of our God;
Whereby the dayspring from on high hath visited us,
To give light to them that sit in darkness
and in the shadow of death,
to guide our feet into the way of peace.

T. Who is the speaker of this passage?

P. Zacharias, a priest of the course of Abia.

T. What "glad tidings" did he receive?

P. Gabriel brought him word that he would be the father of John.

And many of the children of Israel shall he turn to the Lord their God.

And he shall go before him in the spirit and power of Elias, to turn the hearts of the fathers to the children, and the disobedient to the wisdom of the just; to make ready a people prepared for the Lord.

Luke 1. 16, 17.

T. Gabriel said to Mary:

Hail, thou that art highly favoured, the Lord is with thee: blessed art thou among women.

Luke 1. 28.

Why?

P. Mary was chosen to be the mother of Jesus.

He shall be great, and shall be called the Son of the Highest: and the Lord God shall give unto him the throne of his father David.

And he shall reign over the house of Jacob for ever; and of his kingdom there shall be no end.

Luke 1. 32, 33.

T. What distinction is drawn in this chapter between John and Jesus?

P. John is born into the house of the priests; Jesus into the house of the kings.

P. John is to go before Jesus "to make ready a people prepared for the Lord". Jesus is the Son of the Highest and is to reign on the throne of David forever.

T. What is the difference between the *Benedictus* in your literature texts and the Bible version?

P. In the textbook the verses are arranged without numbers and in the form of poetry.

P. Some lines do not begin with capital letters.

T. Which do begin with capitals?

P. Those that begin the verses in the Biblical version.

T. The verses are arranged here in rhythmic patterns. How many accents or beats are there per line?

P. Some lines have four beats; some have three; a few are irregular.

> /   / /   /
> Blessed be the Lord God of Israel
>   /   /   /
> for he hath visited and redeemed his people,
>   /   /   / /
> And hath raised up an horn of salvation for us
>   /   /
> in the house of his servant David;

T. What is the relation of line 2 to 1 and line 4 to 3?

P. The second line in each case is an extension or expression of the thought of the first.

T. In rhythm it sounds like an overflow and can be read with antiphonal effect. How would you classify the words with which the lines begin?

P. Many of the words are connectives, conjunctions, prepositions and the like.

T. What purpose do they serve?

P. They help to preserve the sequence of thought that runs through this intricate pattern.

T. How many complete sentences compose the passage?

P. Two.

T. What is the difference between them?

P. The second is more particular than the first.

P. In the first Zacharias speaks to and for the people; in the second he speaks to the child and for the benefit of the people.

T. What difference is there in tense?

P. The first sentence is in the past tense and tells what the Lord has done; the second is in the future tense and tells what the child will do.

T. With what feelings does Zacharias speak?

P. He speaks with strong and deep feelings of praise and thanksgiving to God for all that He has done.

T. His personal thankfulness becomes the source and occasion of a hymn (a canticle) of national praise. How does the first word reveal the speaker?

P. "Blessed" is the first word that has passed his lips in months, and it expresses in one sudden exclamation his whole attitude and the powerful emotions that have been welling up within this holy man.

P. He is lifted up in spirit.

T. What thoughts direct his mood in the first four lines?

P. His first thought is of God who has remembered His people; and then he thinks of the "Son of the Highest" to be born to Mary and to rule forever on the throne of David. A lesser man would probably have thought of himself or his own son first.

T. What is the distinction in meaning between "visited" and "redeemed"?

P. God has not only visited His people in the presence of His angel Gabriel, but has taken steps to deliver them from sin and damnation.

T. Why is it appropriate that he should refer to Jesus as "an horn of salvation"?

P. He is thinking of Him as an abundant and mighty source of healing.

T. In his great faith Zacharias was already thinking of Jesus, *Ps.* cxxxII, 17, 18, as the mighty deliverer. Why is *horn* a better word here than, say, *method*?

P. It suggests the horn of plenty, and is consequently a clear, concrete and familiar image.

T. Similarly in the next line "in the house" is more vivid than, say, among the people.

And again, observe the use of the word "mouth" in

> As he spake by the mouth of his holy prophets,
> Which have been since the world began:

Zacharias was speaking in a mood of great spiritual exaltation. With what authority did he speak?

P. He spoke of the coming of the Redeemer with a conviction similar to that of all the holy prophets who had preceded him.

T. This gift of prophecy had had a long history.

> Behold the days come, saith the Lord, that I will raise unto David a righteous Branch, and a king shall reign and prosper, and shall execute judgment and justice in the earth.   *Jer.* xxiii. 5.

Why hath God "raised up an horn of salvation for us"?
P.

> That we should be saved from our enemies,
> and from the hand of all that hate us;
> To perform the mercy promised to our fathers,
> and to remember his holy covenant;

T. What had God promised?

P. He had promised to deliver them from fear and to show them mercy.

P. "Hand" is another example of a simple but definite image; it is clearer, for instance, than the word "anger".

T. A covenant is an agreement between two parties. Who are the parties to this holy covenant?

P. God and His chosen people.

T. When had this covenant been made? (See *Gen.* XII. 2, 3.)

P.

And I will make of thee a great nation, and I will bless thee, and make thy name great; and thou shalt be a blessing. And I will bless thee, and curse him that curseth thee: and in thee shall all families of the earth be blessed. *Gen.* XII. 2, 3.

T. What vow had God made to Abraham according to our text?

P.

The oath which he sware to our father Abraham,
That he would grant unto us, that we being delivered
    out of the hand of our enemies
might serve him without fear,
    In holiness and righteousness before him,
all the days of our life.

T. What was God's part of the covenant?

P. He promised to deliver the people from their enemies and from fear of persecution by their enemies, so that they could live in peace.

T. What was the peoples' part of the covenant?

P. We are to serve Him all the days of our life.

T. What is the distinction in meaning between "holiness" and "righteousness"?

P. I do not see any. Do they not both mean goodness?

T. Yes, *holiness* or *sanctity* usually has a personal application. To what relationships might righteousness refer?

P. It might refer to man's relationship to his fellowmen.

T. It could be applied to the laws and covenants that obtain in man's social relationships. In *Jer.* xxiii. 6, the prophet calls the king who shall come to rule over Israel, *The Lord Our Righteousness.* Why, then, does Zacharias exclaim "Blessed is the Lord God of Israel?"

P. God has kept his promise to Abraham and his children according to all the prophecies and is sending a king to rule forever over a righteous people.

T. How is the meaning throughout the passage reinforced by its form and structure?

P. The parallel structure helps to clarify the thought and to make the meaning effective.

T. Antiphonal reading still further heightens the emotional effect. How does this passage differ from most of the poetry you study?

P. This is without rhyme and without any regular number of unaccented syllables per foot.

T. What do these conditions contribute?

P. They permit the rhythmic pattern to follow and support the feelings of the speaker. The absence of rhyme is unnoticed because of the impressiveness of the theme.

T. Under the burden of his prophecy he turns to address his son. Why does he address him?

P. John the Baptist is the one chosen immediately to precede Jesus and to prepare the people for his coming.

And thou, child, shalt be called the prophet of the Highest: for thou shalt go before the face of the Lord to prepare his ways;

T. Why is "face" a better word than "presence", for instance?

P. It is a more clearly defined image.

T. What is gained by the use of images like these— mouth, hand, face, and feet?

P. They have a child-like simplicity, clarity, and familiarity in the midst of these profound utterances. They steady the thought.

T. According to Zacharias what else is John the Baptist to do?

P.

To give knowledge of salvation unto his people
by the remission of their sins,
Through the tender mercy of our God;

T. How are the people to acquire this knowledge?

P. By the confession of their sins.

T. But does not remission mean more than confession?

P. The people receive knowledge of salvation by receiving forgiveness for their sins.

T. Apparently these conditions "knowledge of salvation" and "remission of their sins" are closely connected. On what does forgiveness depend?

P. On the mercy of God.

Whereby the dayspring from on high hath visited us,
    To give light to them that sit in darkness
and in the shadow of death,
to guide our feet into the way of peace.

T. If dayspring is taken literally to mean sunrise, how may the remainder of the passage be interpreted?

P. On account of God's mercy the sun gives light to those who sit helpless in darkness and shadow in order that they may find their way without stumbling.

T. How may the passage be interpreted, if dayspring is taken to mean God?

P. On account of God's mercy He visits us (in the presence of Gabriel and the person of Jesus) to give knowledge of salvation to those in the darkness of ignorance and the shadow of hopelessness that we may find eternal life.

T. How can you show that Zacharias was a man of great faith and zeal?

P. The thought uppermost in his mind is the everlasting mercy of God.

P. In addressing his son he speaks fervently of things to come through God's remembrance of His people.

T. The progress of his passion may be traced in this passage from God to the prophets, to prophecy, to the oath, to the people, to the child, to promises for the future. How is the second sentence connected with the first in the mind of the speaker?

P. Zacharias sees John, the prophet of the Highest at the end or climax of a long succession of prophets who have in turn prophesied the coming of the promised redeemer.

T. This is consistent with the ancient belief in the transmission of wisdom and prophecy through individual men. Zacharias spoke to the people and for the people and expressed not only his own faith but also a belief that was a race tradition. In 1611 an anonymous English poet translated this passage from the Greek of St. Luke. In addition to the meaning of the original what did that translator succeed in preserving?

PP. (*A composite answer.*) He preserved its pentrating directness, simplicity and brevity, majesty and passion.

The images are bold and clear. The music of the rhythm haunts the mind. It is tender and wistful and yearning.

T. The rhythm alone persuades the mind where reason falters. This is a passage of the noblest English: please read it aloud.

T. The title *Benedictus* may be interpreted as a *Blessing invoked.* It is taken from the first word of the Latin version of the canticle. The English is *Blessed.*

If the *Magnificat* has already been studied, the *Benedictus* might very profitably be compared with it.

This passage can now be easily memorized.

Chapter Fifteen

POINTS OF VIEW

<small>SONG OF THE EMIGRANTS IN BERMUDA</small>
Where the remote Bermudas ride
In the ocean's bosom unespied,
From a small boat that rowed along
The listening winds received this song:

"What should we do but sing His praise
That led us through the watery maze
Where He the huge sea-monsters wracks,
That lift the deep upon their backs,
Unto an isle so long unknown,
And yet far kinder than our own?
He lands us on a grassy stage,
Safe from the storms, and prelates' rage:
He gave us this eternal spring
Which here enamels everything,
And sends the fowls to us in care
On daily visits through the air:
He hangs in shades the orange bright
Like golden lamps in a green night,
And does in the pomegranates close
Jewels more rich than Ormuz shows:
He makes the figs our mouths to meet
And throws the melons at our feet;
But apples plants of such a price,
No tree could ever bear them twice.
With cedars chosen by His hand
From Lebanon He stores the land;
And makes the hollow seas that roar
Proclaim the ambergris on shore.
He cast (of which we rather boast)
The Gospel's pearl upon our coast;
And in these rocks for us did frame

230

A temple where to sound His name.
O, let our voice His praise exalt
Till it arrive at Heaven's vault,
Which thence (perhaps) rebounding may
Echo beyond the Mexique bay!"

—Thus sung they in the English boat
A holy and a cheerful note:
And all the way, to guide their chime,
With falling oars they kept the time.[1]

The following suggestions and comments are intended to be used as guides to young teachers who are trying to practise methods similar to those herein recommended. With much of this material provided, they should be free to concentrate on the development of their method.

Before referring to this poem, take up briefly the impressions of Bermuda that the pupils have derived from books, advertisements, travellers, or their imaginations. Against these impressions read aloud this song in such a way that the cadence of the octosyllabics brings out the effect intended and suggested by the line,

With falling oars they kept the time.

How do Marvell's impressions of Bermuda differ from ours? He saw Bermuda as a place of refuge for persecuted Puritans in the middle of the 17th century.

Through whose eyes did he see it? Through the eyes of Puritan friends, "emigrants" who had been there and had told him about it.

Why is it appropriately called a song? It is a paean of praise, a hymn of thanksgiving to God for His abundant blessings to them. Marvell has captured their spirit and

[1] Andrew Marvell.

point of view as they "sing His praise". He actually attributes his words to them by appearing to quote their speech, and refers to God by *He* or *His* eleven times as they recount their blessings.

In this poem Marvell wrote from the reported evidence of friends, but under the compulsion of his own emotions and the direction of his own imagination. Where in the first line of the poem is there evidence of his active imagination? "Ride" suggests that he imagined the distant Bermudas riding like ships at anchor and unnoticed in the shelter of a mighty harbour. (Refer to a map for your own benefit.)

Now quote the opening four lines, "Where the remote . . . received this song."

What further evidence can be found in these lines that he imagined the Puritans in a place of safety and freedom? They were free and safe to row from place to place as they visited with one another or assembled at a meeting-place, and they could sing their praises freely without interference from anyone or fear that the winds might betray them to enemies. (Take up the effect of the inverted structure.)

"What should we . . . than our own?"

For what are they grateful? For God's deliverance, protection, and preservation from religious persecution, shipwreck, and the dangers of uncharted seas. (Take up origin and effect of diction, "maze" and "wracks".) They are grateful that He has brought them to a friendlier isle than England. "Should" suggests that their gratitude was spontaneous, abounding, and uncalculated.

Throughout the study emphasis should be placed at every opportunity on the contrasts between their life in Bermuda and their previous life in England. These contrasts are heightened by Marvell's imagination.

"Grassy stage" refers to some natural and inviting landing-stage where they are "safe" from both physical and spiritual storms.

"Prelates' rage" is an uncomplimentary reference to such high churchmen as Bishop Laud.

In this place of "eternal spring", everything is unusually bright and colourful, as if especially prepared ("enamels") or gilded. Marvell may have been told that some of the colours in the west are higher in tone than the same colours in England.

In His "care" of them, God sends both fowl and fruits in great abundance.

In the passage "He hangs in shades . . . ambergris on shore," attention should be drawn, by questioning, to Marvell's quaint images, fancies, contrasts, and comparisons, and to the crispness of his stiff lyric rhythm, the neatness of his exact rhymes, and the vigour of his pointed inversions. Refer to the dictionary for pronunciation of "pomegranates" and "ambergris". Outside the reefs surrounding the Bermudas are common meeting-places for whales; and sick whales are often seen in that vicinity.

The "orange bright" is a reference to a small yellow fruit similar to the orange as we know it; and the apple "plants" may refer to pineapples. They were so perfect that they could not be surpassed. "Close" suggests a treasure chest.

"He stores the land," and consequently they are no longer dependent on the merchant princes of England for sustenance.

Even the sea is benevolent and bears them benefits. Comment on the 17th century use of "proclaim".

What evidence is given that the Puritans were people of fine tastes and endowments?

"He cast . . . His name."

In this passage "rather" reveals a little Puritan smugness. They had brought the gospel, "a pearl of great price", with them, but in their gratitude to God for deliverance they preferred to give the credit to Him.

"These rocks" probably refers to what have since become known as the Cathedral Rocks (Carveth Wells, *Bermuda in Three Colours*).

"O, let our voice . . . Mexique bay."

This apostrophe shows the intensity of their feeling, the scope of their praise and devotion; and it expresses in a few words their faith ("exalt"), humility ("perhaps"), and hope ("may echo"). In all they are earnest and devout.

"Thus sung they . . . kept the time."

With these closing lines the emotion returns to a normal pitch. The song may be recapitulated under the two words,

A *holy* and a *cheerful* note.

To what does this poem owe its abiding charm? The warmth and intensity of Marvell's sympathy with the emigrants dominates and unifies the emotion of the poem. The whole conception is projected on one horizon of the imagination. The poem is unified by His blessings and their gratitude. It is a hymn, a sincere thanksgiving. "The compactness of the style is as hard as a nut." Within the form of its rigid shell there are passages of dainty and delicate description.

Song from *Rokeby*, Canto Third

"A weary lot is thine, fair maid,
    A weary lot is thine!
To pull the thorn thy brow to braid,
    And press the rue for wine!
A lightsome eye, a soldier's mien,
    A feather of the blue,
A doublet of the Lincoln green,—
    No more of me you knew
      My love!
    No more of me you knew.

"This morn is merry June, I trow,
    The rose is budding fain;
But she shall bloom in winter snow,
    Ere we two meet again."
He turned his charger as he spake,
    Upon the river shore,
He gave his bridle-reins a shake,
    Said "Adieu for evermore,
      My love!
    And Adieu for evermore."[1]

A casual reader may dismiss this poem as trite and insignificant, assuming that the speaker is a freebooter, a proud and arrogant soldier, who has played with the affections of many women, and who speaks the words "My Love" ironically. Such an interpretation reflects a

[1] Sir Walter Scott.

subtle sophistication that is foreign to the poetry of Sir Walter Scott and a superciliousness that is the familiar pastime of those who jump to self-expressive conclusions. It shows a lack of appreciation of the poetry of Brignall Banks and Gretna Green. But in this twentieth century the aim seems to be to force one's own thoughts on the poem rather than to permit one's thoughts to be shaped by the poem.

A safer clue to the central mood and meaning of this poem may be found in the last stanza of Lovelace's *To Lucasta, on Going to the Wars.*

> Yet this inconstancy is such
>   As you too shall adore;
> I could not love thee, Dear, so much
>   Loved I not Honour more.

The speakers in both poems express somewhat similar feelings. For them the call of duty is stronger than the call of love. The speaker in Scott's poem implies that his forester's costume may be the disguise of an outlaw or of a member of a hostile band. This, however, is only hinted at; the main point is that this man and this woman have fallen in love with each other, and naturally, without thought of the consequences. Now with regret and complete awareness of the sacrifice and sorrow that is to be her lot, he makes a clear-cut decision to return whence he had come, before it is too late for both of them. His own sorrow is the unnamed burden of the song, but is suggested by "My Love!" "My Love!" The mood of this lyric is more significant than any action that may be inferred from the slight narrative. Its tender pathos is genuine and is intensified by the aptness to the song itself of the images, sounds, rhythms, and form of the poem. When in *Rokeby* the minstrel ends his song, the narrative continues

> 'What youth is this, your band among,
> The best for minstrelsy and song?
> In his wild notes seem aptly met
> A strain of pleasure and regret.'

In what bad taste is the snap judgment of the sophisticated reader!

In its original setting this lyric is entitled simply "Song", but some ingenious modern anthologists have given it the title *The Rover*. Nothing could be more misleading, unless it be to give it the title *The Ranger*.

Spectator or Participant

There is a fairly common practice among teachers to become spectators rather than participants in the study of poetry. This attitude of detached speculation often leads to serious errors in interpretation. A teacher who has little respect for facts will introduce Keats's *Endymion* as the means of a young poet's escape to beauty from the burdens of social ostracism, ill health, bereavement, and a hopeless love affair. A knowledge of the facts of Keats's life and poetry would prevent such blundering and might stimulate the teacher to look more deeply into the poem and into life. In order to teach one thing well a teacher needs to know a great many.

What possible excuse can be found for a teacher who interprets Gray's *On the Death of a Favourite Cat* from the point of view that the cat fell from a vase into an artificial *lake* in a *beautiful* English garden? What hope can be found for the teaching of poetry when some teachers persist in interpreting Marjorie Pickthall's *The Little Sister of the Prophet* from the point of view that the prophet is dead and the little sister is trying to win him back in spirit to dwell with her? How morbid is the imagination that concocts this fiction! Whither has flown the sense of hearing of a teacher who reads the line from Tennyson's *Northern Farmer* (*New Style*) with the following accents?

Proputty, proputty, proputty—that's what I 'ears em saay

Which is more valuable—to spend the class period trying to prove that Gay's *The Peacock, The Turkey, and the Goose* is a fable or trying to interpret the aptness of its artistry as a fable used to make sardonic comment on human conduct through the self-revealing expressions of these creatures?

Many more examples of carelessness or lack of insight might be given. These, however, should suffice to warn teachers of the need for great care in preparing themselves to meet the responsibilities of tomorrow. If we are not participants at life's feast, our pupils will grow up to be half-hearted spectators undernourished of the bread of life.

Chapter Sixteen

EXPERIENCING DRAMA

THE appeal of any work of art is individual and direct. The chief function of the teacher is to guarantee that the appeal arises from its inner source and that it flows through channels that keep it personal, immediate, and unencumbered. Remembering that in the end the real teachers of literature are the creators of the inspired masterpieces of literary art, the teacher is mainly concerned with stimulating the imagination, sharpening the insight, and strengthening the understanding through orderly thinking, without ever losing sight of the source of appeal. In the teaching of a Shakespearian play this source appears to be twofold—drama and poetry. "Shakespeare the dramatist was absolutely inseparable from Shakespeare the poet."[1] Through an engaging naïveté of dramatic technique and a delicate precision in the poetic use of words, Shakespeare appeals to what is common to all men. A teacher, charged with the responsibility of introducing boys and girls to Shakespeare, must keep attention fixed at once on both the drama and the poetry. "We are not all Mogul diamonds, to take the light," but the appeal is in the play rather than in the notes at the front or the back of the text. Dramatic experience, latent in one of Shakespeare's plays, will not be found in Holinshed's *Chronicle,* Plutarch's *Lives,* Lamb's *Tales,* the history of witchcraft and superstition, the evolution of the

[1] M. C. Bradbrook, *Elizabethan Stage Conditions.* Cambridge.

239

Elizabethan theatre, the refurbished notes of someone's lecture, or the abstractions and calculations of a critic's commentary. "The play's the thing"; go, then, directly to the play!

Begin by reading the play in its entirety. Parts cannot be fully appreciated until the whole has been surveyed. As this first reading proceeds, the scenes should be discussed extensively. After a first *dramatic reading* of the opening scene of *Twelfth Night,* for instance, discussion might take the following course:

Where is Illyria? (A location intentionally vague— imaginary rather than geographical.)

What is wrong with the Duke? (Love-sick.)

How ill is he? (Consumed by passion for Olivia.)

What is his state of mind?

Whence comes Valentine?

Why had the Duke not gone himself to Olivia? (That might have forced a decision, and the Duke is enjoying the suspense.)

What reply does he receive? (She is in seven years' mourning for her brother.)

What effect has her refusal on his ardour?

How does he interpret it?

How can we account for such an interpretation? (Anything can happen in Illyria.)

Where does the Duke go from here? (To seek love thoughts among the flowers.)

How apparently is love going to be treated in this play? (Poetically and playfully—a romantic comedy.)

Why are we interested?

In a first reading only the broad outlines of plot, character, and dramatic purposes are sought. When it is finished, the climax should be determined, and a graph of the rising and falling action plotted to invite the contemplation of the play as a whole and the relative significance of the characters in the action. The foundation for intensive study is now firmly laid.

As the intensive study proceeds, either the teacher or a pupil reads aloud dramatically the passage that is under discussion. The division into scenes, as illustrated in any textbook, is an arbitrary convention that should not be allowed to shape the method of study. A "scene" in Shakespeare often consists of a series of short successive actions. It is usually convenient to study the play in these short dramatic units. During intensive study, for instance, the best time to take up the dramatic purposes of a short action such as *Julius Caesar* Act I, Scene II, ll. 1-11 or ll. 12-24, is at line 11 or line 24, or perchance at line 31, rather than at the end of the "scene", at line 327. The dramatic purposes should include all the significant points in characterization and dramatic action that have been discovered in the study of the "scene" or the passage in itself and in its context.

These short actions are significant as well for the *time* at which they occur in the sequence of the drama. Drama is constantly on the move either to or from a climax of action. To experience drama one must see it in imagination, enter into it emotionally, feel its atmosphere, and encounter the spirit that has its being in the living organism. It is a dynamic process rather than a static product. At any given moment the apparent purpose may be to reveal motives, sow the germs of opinion, or flash a character concept on the screen of the reader's imagination. Shakespeare's power to compel response is so various that it is dangerous to stress too much any one quality or purpose. Analysis must be followed by synthesis, and the parts integrated in the process. We must see it whole, taking the drama and the poetry together. Independent of the speakers, the poetry may be important; but it becomes really significant when caught up in the urgency of the action. "Time and the hour runs through the roughest day."

For the high school pupil, however, the quickest and surest way into the drama and the poetry is through a process of imaginative identification. This way is both immediate and personal, and the teacher can assist the pupil in identifying himself imaginatively with the characters by bringing them to life, as the actor does, and by providing them with life-like situations and modern instances and comparisons to facilitate understanding. If they are left frozen in print, they will be as irresponsive as tailor's dummies in a show-window. Introduced by a skilful teacher, who has no ambition to be an elocutionist, these imaginary characters will speak as living creatures, and eventually they may possess more validity for the pupil than the flesh and blood people with whom he rubs shoulders every day. Through them he may see life in long and sustained perspective. His sympathetic insight may thus be deepened and his intuitive understanding broadened to incorporate a wide range of emotional and imaginative experience.

From the play *Macbeth* a pupil should, among other things, get a sympathetic knowing of what it is like to be ridden by a powerful ambition, to follow false gods, to let admiration take the place of faith, to surrender one's soul to the fiendish and cunning forces of evil, and to discover the vanity of temporal power.

To preserve the memorable speech which is Shakespeare, the teacher in his teaching should keep attention fixed on the dramatic poetry in its context of dramatic action. In the corrupt prosaic meaning of a paraphrase there may be some information but there is little dramatic experience. Words should be observed in their contexts. Divorced from their contexts they lose much of their significance and uniqueness.

Not the big words in Shakespeare, but the little ones, are often laden with intended meaning, and part of the duty of the teacher of English is to train the pupil in their recognition.

MACBETH:
                                                 Present fears
    Are less than horrible imaginings:
    My thought, whose murder yet is but fantastical,
    Shakes so my single state of man that function
    Is smother'd in surmise, and nothing is
    But what is not.

In the study of this passage, for example, the teacher who does not understand the play or his own function in the teaching of it becomes confused by the presence of big words and strange expressions and proceeds to goad the class with such dull questions as the following: What is the meaning of fantastical? What is Macbeth's "single state of man"? What does function mean? What does he mean by surmise? And having thus belaboured the class and reduced the passage to rubble, he passes on without discovering that the central image in the "thought" of this most imaginative man is the murder of Duncan. In the light of what precedes and follows, this is a startling revelation of Macbeth at this particular moment in the sequence. If the teacher will keep his eye focused on the drama going on beneath the words, the gist of meaning latent in the context, the words themselves will come without being called, and they will bring with them, as the need arises, all the meaning and significance that the imaginative reader can comprehend. Words become flesh when their meaning depends on the drama they portray; but drama is lifeless when its action depends alone on the definitive meaning of words.

LADY MACBETH:
                                    O proper stuff!
        This is the very painting of your fear:
        This is the air drawn dagger which, you said,
        Led you to Duncan.

In this passage it is interesting to note Lady Macbeth's flash of insight that fear paints strange images in a disordered mind and her desperation in taunting Macbeth with "air-drawn dagger", but the very simple words "which, you said", that are so often overlooked, turn a flood-light into the darkest recesses of both their characters at this moment. Here is drama, indeed, and food for speculation! When and why had they discussed this matter?

Shakespeare looked at life and saw it whole. If his words appear to fall into their natural speech rhythms with magical precision, the cause may be found as much in the devastating penetration of his insight as· in the unerring sense with which he practised his craft. His spirit moved untrammelled. He felt no urge to revolt against anything, no craze for novelty or originality, no zeal to fulfil a mission. He was in the line of a great tradition, and he left it richer than he found it. He was in his own time as he remains today, the poet of the masses of mankind. Beside him, G. B. Shaw, for instance, is a mere propagandist. Observe the frequency with which Shakespeare is the mouthpiece of his characters and the frequency with which Shaw's characters become the mouthpieces of Shaw's opinions. The best technique the teacher can devise for teaching Shakespeare will never be quite good enough, but for his diligence and skill no workman reaps a higher reward.

Chapter Seventeen

JULIUS CAESAR

EXTENSIVE STUDY (First reading of the drama.)

After reading Scene I, Act I aloud, the teacher may stimulate discussion and gather information by asking questions like the following:

Why have the "commoners" gathered here in the street?

What is a triumph?

What interest, either public or private, have the commoners in this triumph?

Who are the tribunes and what is their status?

What is the attitude of the commoners towards them?

Why do the tribunes set the memory of Pompey against the presence of Caesar?

At the end of the scene what do the tribunes plan to do?

Which tribune assumes the leadership?

What indications are there that conflict may ensue?

Scene II is now read and similarly discussed. When the extensive study of the play is completed, the intensive study begins.

INTENSIVE STUDY

T. (Reading the drama, without naming the speakers.)

FLAVIUS. Hence! home, you idle creatures, get you home;
Is this a holiday? What! Know you not,
Being mechanical, you ought not walk
Upon a labouring day without the sign
Of your profession? Speak, what trade art thou?

FIRST COMMONER. Why, sir, a carpenter.
MARULLUS. Where is thy leather apron, and thy rule?
What dost thou with thy best apparel on?—
You, sir, what trade are you?

Judging by these opening speeches, what is the temper of the play likely to be?

P. A violent conflict may follow these outbursts. The tribunes are annoyed with the people for their disobedience and would reprimand them. Their tone is threatening.

T. What law apparently are they breaking?

P. They are walking in the street without some sign about them to indicate their trade, and this apparently is unlawful except on holidays.

T. How, for instance, should a carpenter appear in the street?

P. Marullus would expect him to wear a leather apron and carry a rule.

T. This was not a Roman law of Caesar's time, but a London police regulation of Shakespeare's time made to aid in the apprehension of vagabonds. Why does Shakespeare introduce it here?

P. The Elizabethan audience would understand its meaning and significance at once.

T. Of whom in our own time do the tribunes remind you?

P. Policemen.

T. From their speeches what distinction can you make between the tribunes?

P. Flavius appears to be the leader. He speaks with the tone of command, but his attitude and his challenge are reasonable. He expects to be obeyed and he is. Marullus, on the other hand, is overbearing, noisy, and unnecessarily severe.

P. Marullus sounds like a bully.

T. To whom does Marullus address his last question?

P. He has been blazing forth at the carpenter, but now he turns to another workman and, imitating Flavius, asks his trade.

T. How would these characters be placed on the stage for dramatic effect?

P. If the commoners were placed on either side of the stage, Marullus could follow Flavius down one side and then sweep with threatening gesture to the other side.

T. Enact this section of the scene to show the contrast in tones, attitudes, and gestures of Flavius and Marullus.

PP. (*Three pupils dramatize the parts of Flavius, Marullus, and the First Commoner.*)

T. The carpenter answered Flavius directly. Now let us see how the second commoner regards Marullus.

SECOND COMMONER. Truly, sir, in respect of a fine workman, I am but, as you would say, a cobbler.

MARULLUS. But what trade art thou? Answer me directly.

SECOND COMMONER. A trade, sir, that I hope I may use with a safe conscience: which is indeed, sir, a mender of bad soles.

MARULLUS. What trade, thou knave? thou naughty knave, what trade?

SECOND COMMONER. Nay, I beseech you, sir, be not out with me: yet, if you be out, sir, I can mend you.

MARULLUS. What meanest thou by that? Mend me, thou saucy fellow!

SECOND COMMONER. Why, sir, cobble you.

FLAVIUS. Thou art a cobbler, art thou?

What is the Second Commoner's attitude towards Marullus?

P. He is not afraid of him, and he is certainly not very respectful. He finds amusement at the expense of Marullus.

T. Why is Marullus piqued by the commoner's first reply?

P. The reply may be interpreted in two ways. The commoner may mean that in comparison with a worker in a fine art he is only a mender of shoes, whereas Marullus probably understands him to mean that in comparison with a good workman he is only a poor or unskilled worker.

T. What effect has this reply on Marullus?

P. It confuses and annoys him and he demands to be answered briefly and "directly".

T. How is he answered the second time?

P. Indirectly. Again the commoner expresses two meanings by punning on *soles*. First he means that as an honest cobbler, following a legitimate trade, he is a mender of shoes, but the other meaning that his words convey makes him a saver (mender) of souls, and in this trade he modestly hopes that he himself will always know right from wrong.

T. What effect has this quibbling on Marullus?

P. It makes him angry, and he flies out at the commoner.

T. How do you know?

P. I can see the commoner, suddenly cringing before Marullus as he exclaims, "Nay, I beseech you, sir, be not out with me."

T. What must the commoner think of Marullus?

P. He must know Marullus for what he is, a dull wit who is easily provoked to anger, an incompetent but officious fellow whose bark is worse than his bite. He had probably met Marullus before, because he quibbles again as he is threatened, and while he proclaims that if Marullus needs his shoes repaired he can mend them, he also insinuates that if Marullus gets out of temper with him he can teach a tribune good manners.

T. What evidence can you find to show that Marullus is exasperated by this reply?

P. He gets on his dignity, "Mend me, thou saucy fellow!"

P. He is so angry that he cannot think straight.

P. Flavius catches on first to the play on the word *cobble,* and puts an end to the commoner's evasion by the question "Thou art a cobbler, art thou?"

T. What further distinction between the two tribunes is drawn by this?

P. Marullus is hot-headed and bombastic. He likes to show his authority and boss people around. Flavius does not bluster and shout. He speaks more respectfully to the people and no one tries to make fun of him. Perhaps, too, he can take a joke. At least, he can see through one.

T. If you were preparing this section of the scene for dramatic presentation, how would you bring out this contrast?

P. First, Marullus should be shorter and stouter than Flavius. If Marullus were portrayed as red-faced and impetuous in speech and act, Flavius, tall and dignified in bearing, should express in tone and gesture both command and understanding of the people.

T. How could the commoners be made to accentuate this contrast?

P. To Flavius, the man, they could show some respect and obedience. In Marullus they should show an amused interest, but for his office neither fear nor respect.

T. What are the chief qualities you would expect the commoners to reveal?

P. They should be portrayed as careless, restless, sometimes clever creatures, ready to follow sport or fortune where it leads. As the cobbler clatters, they laugh noisily at his replies.

T. Read the speeches to reveal these characters.

PP. (*Assigned pupils give a dramatic reading of the passage.*)

T. Let us see if our findings are borne out by what follows.

> FLAVIUS. Thou art a cobbler, art thou?
> SECOND COMMONER. Truly, sir, all that I live by is with the awl: I meddle with no tradesman's matters, nor women's matters, but with awl. I am, indeed, sir, a surgeon to old shoes; when they are in great danger, I re-cover them. As proper men as ever trod upon neat's-leather have gone upon my handywork.
> FLAVIUS. But wherefore art not in thy shop today?
> Why dost thou lead these men about the streets?
> SECOND COMMONER. Truly, sir, to wear out their shoes, to get myself into more work. But indeed, sir, we make holiday to see Caesar, and to rejoice in his triumph.
> MARULLUS. Wherefore rejoice? What conquest brings he home?
> What tributaries follow him to Rome,
> To grace in captive bonds his chariot-wheels?

Is the second commoner really more respectful to Flavius?

P. He persists in quibbling, but he no longer evades the question. "All that I live by is with the awl" is clear enough to anyone who recognizes the awl as the sign of a cobbler's profession. But he cannot resist quibbling on the word *awl,* first to say that meddling with the awl is his only trade, and secondly to suggest that he is not particularly concerned with whose affairs he meddles. Following through with his first meaning he says he is "a surgeon to old shoes". When they are badly worn he patches them and thus restores them again to service. He even shows a little pride in his handiwork.

P. It is true that the cobbler babbles like a brook, but his replies to Flavius perhaps do not provoke the other commoners to as much laughter as his replies to Marullus most certainly do. In his second reply to Flavius he goes straight to the point and reveals to us what we have wanted to know since the first question was asked.

T. Who draws this straightforward answer?

P. Flavius.

T. Who takes advantage of it?

P. Marullus.

T. What mood is he in as he rushes headlong to the attack?

P. He sounds highly indignant with the people because they have come out to see Caesar and to make merry at his triumph.

T. How can the full effect of his indignation be portrayed on the stage?

P. As the cobbler finishes his speech, some of the commoners shout their assent. Then Marullus with voice pitched to mount with his swelling questions cuts in with

> Wherefore rejoice? What conquest brings he home?
> What tributaries follow him to Rome,
> To grace in captive bonds his chariot-wheels?

T. What are some of the causes contributing to the indignation of Marullus?

P. He has been looking for a fight from the beginning. His whole attitude is wrong, and the cobbler, who apparently knew him to be a blithering incompetent whose bark is worse than his bite, takes him for a ride.

T. Your figure of speech "he takes him for a ride" is ill-chosen.

P. Well, he gives him the run-around, or pushes him about.

T. He does neither. Unless figurative language is apt in its context, it is neither illustrative nor idiomatic. There is here no suggestion of riding or running or pushing. An old figure based on the practice of bear-baiting would be apt, since Marullus is not unlike a bear that is baited or teased or worried. What is his chief grievance now that the cobbler has declared himself?

P. Caesar is not entitled to a triumph, he says, because he has conquered no one and has brought no captive rulers to Rome.

T. Among the prerequisites of a triumph was a victory over a foreign enemy. Caesar's pretext for this triumph was the destruction at Munda in Spain of domestic or private enemies, namely the sons of Pompey. Some Romans thought Caesar was not entitled to this triumph, but the common people were apparently more interested in a triumph than in the rights of triumphant leaders. What is the aim of Marullus as he speaks?

Wherefore rejoice? What conquest brings he home?
What tributaries follow him to Rome,
To grace in captive bonds his chariot-wheels?
You blocks, you stones, you worse than senseless things!
O you hard hearts, you cruel men of Rome,
Knew you not Pompey? Many a time and oft
Have you climb'd up to walls and battlements,
To towers and windows, yea, to chimney-tops,
Your infants in your arms, and there have sat
The live-long day, with patient expectation,
To see great Pompey pass the streets of Rome:
And when you saw his chariot but appear,
Have you not made an universal shout,
That Tiber trembled underneath her banks,
To hear the replication of your sounds
Made in her concave shores?
And do you now put on your best attire?
And do you now cull out a holiday?
And do you now strew flowers in his way
That comes in triumph over Pompey's blood?
Be gone!
Run to your houses, fall upon your knees,
Pray to the gods to intermit the plague
That needs must light on this ingratitude.

P. Marullus is trying to turn the people against Caesar.

T. How does he try to achieve this end?

P. First, he raises the question, Is Caesar entitled to a triumph? Then he reminds them of the enthusiasm with which they once celebrated the triumph of the great Pompey, that they may contrast with it their present half-hearted preparations for Caesar's triumph. Caesar, he says, is merely celebrating the defeat of Pompey's sons. Finally he threatens them with a plague for their forgetfulness of the gods.

T. What proof is there that his speech, for all its eloquence, is bombastic and his statements are exaggerated?

P. Contrasted with "you idle creatures" of Flavius,

> You blocks, you stones, you worse than senseless things!
> O you hard hearts, you cruel men of Rome,
> Knew you not Pompey?

is severe and threatening language.

P. Even if the people did all that he says they did, it is impossible to believe that the river trembled when they shouted.

T. Make a diagram to show the course of the sound.

P.

(A few apt strokes on the blackboard will quickly clarify the meaning here.)

T. Why did you show the sound as bounding back and forth on your diagram?

P. It expresses the meaning of "replication", as the echo passes from bank to bank.

T. Read the speech again silently. Is there anything in its structure to indicate that it might be highly emotional in effect?

P. Marullus is apparently devoted to the memory of Pompey. He mentions his name three times.

P. The speech is almost entirely a series of questions arranged in such a way as to arouse the feelings of the commoners. It rises in tempo through a long question surmounted by these three:

> And do you now put on your best attire?
> And do you now cull out a holiday?
> And do you now strew flowers in his way
> That comes in triumph over Pompey's blood?

to break finally in the dramatic climax of "Be gone!"

T. Could this effect be produced as well in prose? Contrast this blank verse with the previous passage of prose.

P. The prose has the chattiness of witty conversation; the blank verse has the continuity of an address.

P. One mood dominates in this long passage of poetry. Both the feeling and the thought flow in swift sequence and rhythm. By contrast prose would be loose and cold and perhaps ineffective. Marullus here is trying to make the formal oration of a commanding officer, but lacking in natural dignity he sounds like a cheap "spellbinder".

T. This type of person is called a demagogue. Now let us see from what follows what effect his rhetorical eloquence has on the commoners. Marullus concludes with

> Run to your houses, fall upon your knees,
> Pray to the gods to intermit the plague
> That needs must light on this ingratitude.

and Flavius appeals to the people with

> Go, go, good countrymen, and, for this fault,
> Assemble all the poor men of your sort;
> Draw them to Tiber banks, and weep your tears
> Into the channel, till the lowest stream
> Do kiss the most exalted shores of all.
>
> (*Exeunt* COMMONERS)

P. When the noisy Marullus finishes speaking, the people stand dumbfounded, wondering what to do. It is Flavius who gets results with his quiet manner and reasonable attitude.

T. Flavius, like Marullus, bases his appeal on the ingratitude of the people. He says "for this fault". But why does he succeed where Marullus fails?

P. He is more direct.

P. Yes, but Marullus has prepared the way for him.

T. Contrast their appeals.

P. Marullus tries to frighten the people. Basing his appeal on a superstition of the time, i.e. that an epidemic might be visited on them for their sins against the gods (among whom he places Pompey), he appeals to their sense of fear. Flavius, on the other hand, assumes that they are contrite and sends them for the remission of their sins to father Tiber, the great river whose spirit flowed through their religion like that of a god. Flavius shows the better understanding of the people and how to handle them. He gives them something to do. They are to gather together all the other commoners and go to the Tiber. This will take them out of the streets. Marullus merely tells these few to go home and pray. Marullus perhaps believes that the commoners are still, like himself, interested in the Roman leaders.

T.

> See, whether their basest metal be not moved;
> They vanish tongue-tied in their guiltiness.

How does Flavius characterize the people?

P. They are a low-spirited, guilty crowd, easily cowed, persuaded and controlled.

T. What would such a crowd probably do if given reasons, plausible or otherwise, why someone should be destroyed?

P. They would set to work blindly and tear him to pieces, just as they do the poet Cinna later. These are the same Romans whom Antony worked his spell upon.

T.

Go you down that way towards the Capitol;
This way will I: disrobe the images,
If you do find them deck'd with ceremonies.
    MARULLUS: May we do so?
You know it is the feast of Lupercal.
    FLAVIUS: It is no matter; let no images
Be hung with Caesar's trophies. I'll about
And drive away the vulgar from the streets:
So do you too where you perceive them thick.
These growing feathers pluck'd from Caesar's wing
Will make him fly an ordinary pitch,
Who else would soar above the view of men
And keep us all in servile fearfulness.

What further interests have these two tribunes in common?

P. Both men wish to detract as much as possible from the success of Caesar's triumph. They have sent some of the people out of the streets, and now they are going into the public squares to remove from monuments and memorials what decorations they can find.

T. At this time Caesar had many images of himself set up in the Capitol. To take such risks, the tribunes must have had real grievances against Caesar.

P. Pompey had increased the number of tribunes, and these two perhaps owed their positions to him. They may feel now that Caesar is getting too strong and would like to free himself from the tribunes' power of veto. Flavius says that Caesar is flying too high.

T. The metaphor here is based on falconry, an Elizabethan method of hunting. The "pitch" is the highest point at which the falcon flies before it sweeps down on its prey. What are the points of comparison in the metaphor as applied to Caesar?

P. Caesar is compared to a young and ambitious falcon that may soon be able to fly to such a "pitch" that all other birds will have good reason to live in fear of it. By taking from the "images" what decorations they can find, the tribunes believe they will divert from Caesar the attention and respect of the people with whom he may become too powerful. They appear to be jealous of Caesar or fearful lest he deprive them of their offices and powers.

T. What contrasts are here noticeable between Flavius and Marullus?

P. Flavius is the senior; Marullus asks questions and Flavius gives commands.

T. Concerning what?

P. Marullus wonders if they are justified in disrobing the images on this day of national purification, the feast of Lupercal, but Flavius, who is surer of himself and of what he thinks is best for the people, sets aside all objections and is intent on doing all that he can to dishonour Caesar in the eyes of the people.

T. What is revealed by the fact that he dares to pursue such a course at this time, the feast of Lupercal?

P. Perhaps Flavius, who has a better understanding of the people, feels that this festival has lost much of its original significance for them. Marullus is a fearful servant of tradition. Flavius, on the other hand, wishes to throw off this attitude of "servile fearfulness" in all things.

T. Marullus and Flavius well represent the difference between the imitator and the instigator of action and the commoners are the fickle dupes of both. What are the dramatic purposes of this scene?

P. It sets off by contrast two Roman tribunes whose common bond is self-interest. They are more anxious to preserve their jobs and play politics than to improve the general welfare.

P. It represents the commoners as a servile, unprincipled mob, more ready to live off the state, or its leaders, than to work for a living and their own independence. They, too, are here to satisfy self-interest.

P. It gives us some hints of the political situation and the social conditions in Rome at this time.

P. It sets the stage for the entrance of Caesar.

T. Why are we particularly interested in him?

P. We wish to see what a Roman emperor looks like, to see for ourselves if he is as ambitious and dangerous as the tribunes make him out to be.

P. We want to see what a triumph looks like and how the people receive Caesar.

P. We wish to know what success the tribunes have had in influencing the people.

P. There are forecasts here of trouble to come; we wish to see what happens.

P. Everybody is interested in a fight.

T. What impression is made on you by the scene as a whole?

P. It is full of foreboding. From the first challenge of Flavius to his last command, our feelings are kept on edge, as it were, by the bickering of the commoner and the noisy oratory of Marullus. When the scene is ended one is left with a feeling of uneasiness and a desire to see what is to follow.

T. If you were preparing this scene for dramatic presentation what types would you choose for various parts. (Keep in mind stature, appearance, manner, and voice.)

PP. (The pupils discuss this problem and choose members of the class to read the parts. Flavius, they think, should be tall and erect in bearing, commanding in appearance, and stern in manner. Marullus should be stout, red-faced, and blustering and bullying in manner. The commoners should be distinguished from one another by height, manner, and voice, but all should bear marks of their defeated condition.)

The study of the scene closes with the dramatization of it in the classroom.

Chapter Eighteen

MACBETH

Act I

Scene 1: *A Desert Place*

Thunder and lightning.   Enter three witches.

1 Witch. When shall we three meet again
In thunder, lightning, or in rain?
2 Witch. When the hurlyburly's done,
When the battle's lost and won. ⸺
3 Witch. That will be ere the set of sun.
1 Witch. Where the place?
2 Witch.   Upon the heath.
3 Witch. There to meet with Macbeth.
1 Witch. I come, Graymalkin.
2 Witch. Paddock calls.
3 Witch. Anon!
All.   Fair is foul, and foul is fair:
Hover through the fog and filthy air.

Exeunt

Extensive Treatment—The first reading of the drama.

T. (After reading the scene aloud as effectively as he can.) As an imaginative member of an audience, what would interest you in this scene?

P. (After reading the scene silently.) I should like to see what witches look like.

T. What do you think they would look like? *(Various pupils describe.)*

T. How would you imagine them to act? to speak? *(Various pupils illustrate.)*

T. What else would interest you?

P. I should like to know what they are doing here, and why they intend to "meet again".

T. Where, apparently, do they usually meet? (*Pupil describes.*)

T. What in this scene arouses your interest in what may follow?

P. We wish to know where, and why, and between whom a battle is being fought.

P. We wish to know who Macbeth is, and what the witches have to do with him.

INTENSIVE TREATMENT—The second reading of the drama.

T. (*After the scene has been read aloud by the teacher or the pupils.*) In a court of law, with what could these witches be charged?

P. They were accessory before the fact.

P. They were guilty of inciting to murder, insanity, and suicide.

P. They sought the ruination not only of Macbeth but of all human society.

T. What appears to be the natural abode of the witches?

P. They were accustomed to meet in deserted places in thunder, lightning, and rain.

P. They are like disembodied spirits that inhabit the air. They can move anywhere at will.

T. How would superstitious people interpret this?

P. Foul deeds might be accompanied by foul weather. Natural storms might be a sign of storms in the moral firmament.

T. What, apparently, has brought them together here?

P. Some evil scheme is under way, and they are plotting its outcome.

T. What distinction can be made between the first and the second witch?

P. The first witch is thinking of what has just taken place, and wishes to meet again. The second witch is thinking of the present battle and its outcome.

T. How do their speeches contrast in sound?

P. The speech of the first witch is a high-pitched, shrill shriek; that of the second is deep and ominous.

T. What is sinister and malicious in the speech of the second witch?

P. The meaning of "lost and won" is evidently clearer to the witches than it is to us. It suggests more than it states.

T. The second witch appears to have an uncanny insight into human affairs. What is suggested by the sound of "hurlyburly"?

P. If the witch thinks of a battle as a confusion of sounds, it is easy to imagine from the way in which this word may be spoken the fiendish delight of the witch in the destruction of mortals.

T. What special power does the third witch possess as revealed in her speech "That will be ere the set of sun"?

P. She has a foreknowledge of the time when the battle will end.

T. What distinction can be made between the first and the third witch?

P. The first asks a question; the third makes an assertion.

P. The first asks for information; the third speaks with the command of a leader.

T. How do their speeches contrast in sound?

P. The speech of the first is in a high pitch and shrill. The sound of the third witch is hard, sharp, and metallic.

T. What is suggested by the rhythm of these lines? Scan them.

P.

```
   /   ⌣   /   ⌣   /   ⌣   /
When shall | we three | meet a | gain |
   ⌣   /   ⌣   /   ⌣   /   ⌣   /
In thun | der light | ning or | in rain? |
   /   ⌣   /   ⌣   /   ⌣   /
When the | hurly | burly's | done |
   /   ⌣   /   ⌣   /   ⌣   /
When the | battle's | lost and | won |
   /   ⌣   /   ⌣   ⌣   /   ⌣   /
That will | be ere | the set | of sun |
```

P. The rhythm of these trochaic tetrametres either suggests or reinforces the weird dance, the demoniac gestures, and the strange gibberish of the witches.

P. The absence of the last syllable necessary to complete the rhythm (in three of the lines) extends abnormally the sound of the single syllable in the last foot, and this produces an effect uncanny and suggestive of the witches' fateful power, working inevitably toward a mysterious end.

P. The rhythm helps to set the pitch for the fiendish incantation of the witches.

T. What is the effect of the rhyme?

P. The rhyming words all contain nasal sounds that can be resonated.

P. The rhymes give the suggestion of fiendish efficiency. "What's done is done."

P. They make the evil power of the witches seem unchallengeable.

T. Who are the attendants or companions of the witches? What company do they keep?

P. "I come, Graymalkin", and "Paddock calls" show that the witches are the obedient servants of evil spirits in animal form.

T. What powers do they possess or assume?

P. They are potentially the instruments of evil.

T. What is the demon interest of the third witch?

P. The third witch assumes already a power over Macbeth. She appears to be her own master—perhaps a leader.

T. What indication is given that they delight in filth and moral perversion?

P.

> Fair is foul, and foul is fair:
> Hover through the fog and filthy air.

They delight in setting in utter confusion all moral values.

T. It may be that they are devoid of human feelings and lack a sense of moral values. How should these lines be sounded?

P. The sound of "f" should be dominant and *breathy*, to give the impression of the exhalation of foul air. In sound these lines should provide in pitch and volume a climax to all that has gone before.

T. In Macbeth's time people believed that these evil creatures had no influence over the will of those who believed in God. In what position would this belief put Macbeth?

P. He would be a man without a strong faith or the will to believe. Apparently he is such a man, and the third witch may intend to lead him on until he destroys himself.

T. What relationship may this scene bear to the drama that follows?

P. It strikes the key-note of the action; it suggests the theme and sets the pitch.

P. It arouses the interest at once.

T. If this is characteristic of Shakespeare's dramatic power, what can be said of it?

P. He can put a great deal in a small space.

P. He can go at once to the heart of his problem.

P. He can awaken the imagination.

P. He can make language produce the effects that he wants.

P. He can create characters.

NOTES AND COMMENTS ON TEACHING DRAMA

Scenes are studied in short actions or units.

Passages are read dramatically as the study progresses.

A general question is used first to ascertain the mood, thought, or purpose of the passage as a whole.

Behind the questioning there is a definitely organized plan, the purpose of which varies with the nature of the material being discussed.

The question-answer sequence affords practice in concentration and clear thinking, and it is through this process that the meaning of the drama gradually makes its advance.

Contrasts, modern illustrations, known situations, and diagrams are used to clarify the action.

Where language needs special attention, words are studied in their contexts.

Wherever metre, rhythm, and form reinforce the meaning, they are integrated with the action or the characterization.

Discussion of dramatic presentation deepens interpretation and furthers the process of imaginative identification.

Before the pupils are assigned parts to be read dramatically, the qualities of character to be portrayed should be discussed.

Recapitulation of a scene should follow naturally from the study of the scene.

The drama should be kept alive as a drama all the time.

Many people say that you spoil great poetry for the young by turning it into a school lesson, but I believe this to be nonsense. If you meet a man who says that he cannot read Shakespeare because he had to learn the plays at school, you may be reasonably sure that the tastes with which he was born lay outside Shakespeare. I doubt whether the taste for poetry can be destroyed by teaching children either good poetry or bad. I sometimes wonder, indeed, whether anything is of very much importance in education except the character of the teacher.[1]

[1] Y. Y. (Robert Lynd): 10,000 *Things*. The *New Statesman and Nation*.

Chapter Nineteen

L'ENVOI

I

IF the departments of English in 'the universities profess that their chief interest and purpose is the liberation of genius for the pursuance of research, the training of the talents of would-be teachers can hardly be expected to come within the range of their ambitions. The time may come very soon when educational authorities will be forced to recruit from the senior forms of the secondary schools a selected number of recommended candidates, and to set up their own college and courses to provide students with the kind of literary background and methods of study necessary for the successful teaching of English.

What it all comes to is that the average cultivated person is spiritualized at the periphery but not at the core. Everything is all right but the foundations. There is sensitiveness, imagination, logicality, urbanity, but no true serenity, and little poise or power. The man at once charms us with his command of the more superficial levels of experience and disappoints us by his failure to deal with fundamentals. His consciousness is not irrigated from the central fount of his being; the sap has not mounted from the roots. Deep down he is the whole time on the defensive. Although he moves freely and confidently about on the plane of ideas he is defenceless against one ray from the solar plexus. Silence discovers him. When he is deprived of his polished intellectual weapons he finds himself unable to compel or persuade. In spite of all his sophistication he is distressed by the sense of a dreadful void within. Although he knows a great deal, what he **is** is something relatively insignificant.

Unfortunately, however, it may take him a long time to realize these things with any completeness. For the very wealth of his superficial knowledge and attainments serves to blind him to the fact that at bottom he is divided against himself. The words of Jesus regarding the rich man's difficulty have here a significant enough application. For between the more highly educated person and the truths which he so urgently needs to know there hangs the richly embroidered curtain of his own sophistication. He has become too sensitive to complexities to be able to perceive the simple. . . .

Distinctive of the body of teaching which is imparted to the students in our universities is the fact that it can be assimilated, organized, and formulated without any really serious demands being made upon their powers of introspection. They are never required, in order to verify or identify their conclusions, to look really deeply within. Or let us say, rather that they are never required to undertake any exploration which is likely to involve them in spiritual uneasiness or distress. If they do, the result is only that they bewilder their examiners. They are normally occupied in handling data which have been created by abstracting from the individual situation certain relatively simple features which lend themselves to forming a point of departure for abstract theorizing. And the result is that the values which they acquire by this process are not the values which really tell, not the values which provide them with any real command over their experiences.[1]

The intellectualized treatment of literature bears to the experiencing of poetry about the same relation as the study of geography from maps of British Columbia bears to personal travel through the Rocky Mountains. The one tests the endurance of a drudge; the other quickens his spirit as he lifts up his eyes unto the hills, and his mind, perchance, to God.

The question is, how long can we afford the exclusive luxury of academic isolation?

II

Who are the Blimps? J. B. Priestley has unctuously applied the term to the social aristocrats in England who are being wiped out by the war. When this process of

[1] Lawrence Hyde, *The Prospects of Humanism.*

wiping out has been completed, it is assumed that victory over all our enemies will at last be in sight. The term Blimp can be applied as well to Mr. Priestley. The whole group of socialist adventurers is like a flock of Blimps floating comfortably aloof in the pleasant on-shore breeze of its own exuberance, and waiting to descend when political advantage is opportune:

> Stationed always in the skies
> Waiting for the flesh that dies.[1]

While the intellectuals are playing golf or bridge, other men are preparing to defend the nation. When the war is over the intellectuals, you may be sure, will all be able to answer to their names at roll-call. The fact is Blimps may be found in any sky—whether it be social, political, educational, or religious. The question is, Who are the Blimps?

III

Who should control the courses of study in English in the secondary school? Should the courses be constructed on horizontal planes or in a graded vertical core? Should the aim be only to increase literary information or to deepen insight and extend experience? Should the purpose be to suggest the reading of a larger amount of material for the superficial exploration of the subject, or to invite the study of a smaller amount with imaginative penetration? Who are likely to know the correct answers to these questions?

IV

Very few teachers of mathematics would venture to go before a class without a clear idea of the solution of all the problems of a lesson. Certainly not all teachers of English

[1] Ralph Hodgson, *The Bull.*

face their classes with a clear idea of what they intend to achieve, or all the meaning and significance of what they expect to teach. It is just that margin of bluff and balderdash that makes it possible for an incompetent teacher of English to escape discovery by himself or his pupils for a long time. Both soon become inured to superficialities, and the pathos of the situation is deepened by the fact that both think they are getting something. The solution of this problem is not so easy as it may appear to some people.

v

Since teachers with any degree of scholarship, training, and aptitude in English may be appointed to teach the subject, it is to be expected that the quality of the teaching will vary greatly from school to school, even from class to class. Only by teaching, however, can the teacher find his power or reveal his lack of it. Is it possible, then, that some teachers may profit by a refresher course in the materials and the methods of study in English? Some people will ask, Is it not time that the whole system of selection, training, and appointment of teachers were overhauled? The answers to these questions will afford only partial solutions, unless opinions like the following are taken into account.

There is a common English phrase, 'the right man in the right place.' To which we might rejoin, 'Cobbler, to thy last!' Who knows what is the post that suits him best and for which he is most fitted? Does a man himself know it better than others or do they know it better than he? Who can measure capacities and aptitudes? The religious attitude, undoubtedly, is to endeavour to make the occupation in which we find ourselves our vocation, and only in the last resort to change it for another.[1]

[1] Miguel de Unamuno, *The Tragic Sense of Life*. By permission of Macmillan & Co. Ltd.

'Do the duty which lies nearest thee,' which thou knowest to be a Duty! Thy second Duty will already have become clearer.[1]

This was Carlyle's gospel of work—"to know what God bids thee do, and to do it."[1]

VI

The modern town-dweller has no God and no Devil; he lives without awe, without admiration, without fear.[1]

We are all born humanists; the poet is among the foremost of men who can help us to transcend our birthright. Through his art he may purge the feelings, clarify the thoughts, and sharpen the sword of the spirit. When the world finds peace again, it will have rediscovered, it is hoped, the serenity of the poet and his belief in the eternal verities—faith and wonder and humility. What, then, can poetry offer the pilgrim who earnestly seeks her shrine?

[1] Thomas Carlyle, *Sartor Resartus.*
[2] William Ralph Inge, *Outspoken Essays.*

Chapter Twenty

A BIBLIOGRAPHY

In the construction and development of the theme presented in this book, the following have played a part:

I—PHILOSOPHY AND EDUCATION

Karl Barth: *The Word of God and the Word of Man*. Hodder, 1929.
Nicolas Berdyaev: *The End of Our Time*. Bles.
――*The Meaning of History*. Bles, 1936.
――*Solitude and Society*. Bles, 1938.
H. Emil Brunner: *The Theology of Crisis*. Scribner, 1929.
Alexis Carrel: *Man, the Unknown*. Harper, 1935.
F. Clarke: *Education and Social Change*. Sheldon, 1940.
Sidney Dark: *Orthodoxy Sees It Through*. Barker.
Christopher Dawson: *Religion and the Modern State*. Sheed, 1935.
W. Macneile Dixon: *The Human Situation*. E. Arnold, 1938.
Charles Gore: *Belief in God*. Murray, 1921.
T. E. Hulme: *Speculations*. Kegan Paul, 1924.
Lawrence Hyde: *The Learned Knife*. Howe, 1929.
   (This book shows the limitations of the sociologist's efforts.)
Lawrence Hyde: *The Prospects of Humanism*. Howe, 1931.
   (This book presents the blind spots in the humanistic point of view.)
Carl Gustav Jung: *Psychology and Religion*. Yale, 1938.
Jacques Maritain: *Art and Scholasticism*. Sheed, 1930.
――*True Humanism*. Sheed, 1938.
Viscount Samuel: *Belief and Action*. Cassell, 1937.
Miguel de Unamuno: *The Tragic Sense of Life*. Macmillan, 1939.

II—LITERATURE AND EDUCATION

Lascelles Abercrombie: *Poetry: Its Music and Meaning*. Oxford, 1932.
S. Alexander: *Beauty and Other Forms of Value*. Macmillan, 1933.
Owen Barfield: *Poetic Diction*. Faber, 1928.
Clive Bell: *Art*. Chatto, 1914.

M. C. Bradbrook: *Elizabethan Stage Conditions*. Cambridge, 1932.
(This book presents a criticism of the criticism of Shakespeare.)
Robert Bridges: *The Necessity of Poetry*. Oxford, 1917.
Stephen J. Brown: *The Realm of Poetry*. Harrap, 1921.
John Drinkwater: *The Lyric*. Secker, 1922.
T. S. Eliot: *The Sacred Wood*. Methuen, 1920.
　　　　The Use of Poetry and the Use of Criticism. Faber, 1933.
William Empson: *Seven Types of Ambiguity*. Chatto, 1934.
Roger Fry: *Vision and Design*. Chatto, 1920.
H. W. Garrod: *The Profession of Poetry*. Oxford, 1929.
P. Gurrey: *The Appreciation of Poetry*. Oxford, 1935.
G. Rostrevor Hamilton: *Poetry and Contemplation*. Cambridge, 1937.
(This book presents a criticism of I. A. Richards' practices.)
L. S. Harris: *The Nature of English Poetry*. Dent, 1931.
Aldous Huxley: *Texts and Pretexts*. Chatto, 1932.
Frank Kendon: *The Adventure of Poetry*. Black, 1932.
F. R. Leavis: *New Bearings in English Poetry*. Chatto, 1932.
F. R. Leavis and Denys Thompson: *Culture and Environment*.
Chatto, 1934.
John Livingston Lowes: *The Road to Xanadu*. Houghton, 1927.
P. H. B. Lyon: *The Discovery of Poetry*. E. Arnold, 1930.
Stephen Potter: *The Muse in Chains*. Cape, 1937.
Ernest Raymond: *Through Literature to Life*. Cassell, 1938.
I. A. Richards: *Practical Criticism*. Kegan Paul, 1929.
　　　　The Principles of Literary Criticism. Kegan Paul, 1934.
(This book reveals what may happen when the methods and
practices of psychology are applied to the study of literature.)
　　　　Science and Poetry. Kegan Paul, 1926.
M. R. Ridley: *Poetry and the Ordinary Reader*. Dent, 1938.
George H. W. Rylands: *Words and Poetry*. Hogarth, 1928.
John Sparrow: *Sense and Poetry*. Constable, 1934.
Denys Thompson: *Reading and Discrimination*. Chatto, 1934.
E. M. W. Tillyard: *Poetry Direct and Oblique*. Chatto, 1934.
Charles Williams: *The English Poetic Mind*. Oxford, 1932.